Visitors along My Cancer Journey

Emotional Release of Generational Wounds

KLAZINA DOBBE

BALBOA
PRESS

A DIVISION OF HAY HOUSE

Balboa Press books may be ordered through booksellers or by contacting:

Balboa Press
A Division of Hay House
1663 Liberty Drive
Bloomington, IN 47403
www.balboapress.com
1 (877) 407-4847

Print information available on the last page.

ISBN: 978-1-5043-9834-3 (sc)
ISBN: 978-1-5043-9835-0 (hc)
ISBN: 978-1-5043-9842-8 (e)

Library of Congress Control Number: 2018902056

Balboa Press rev. date: 02/26/2018

In memory of my Oma

Contents

Contents

Preface

The Journey

Nothing could have prepared me for the moment I learned I had cancer. Such a diagnosis was only happening to others, I thought. Never did I suspect that one day it would be mine.

At the first declaration of the possibility I might have breast cancer, I was shaken to the core of my being. The call came four days after a routine mammogram, informing me of "a suspicious density that needed to be examined." After the initial shock, a tsunami of fearful emotions and thoughts flooded my entire being. In my panic, questions surfaced, leading me to places I did not want to go.

These questions included, What if I have cancer? What will happen to me? Will I live or die? And how will my family deal with this diagnosis?

Only a couple of months before I learned about my own condition, my sister, Coby, had been diagnosed with brain cancer. She had clusters of tumors in her brain that could not be operated on. The doctors gave her three months to a year to live. How was it possible, I thought, that the only two females in our family of five kids were diagnosed with cancer merely months apart, while living six thousand miles away from each other?

The day before I flew to Holland to be with my sister, my doctor called me to tell me the bad news that I indeed had breast cancer. The following week, we sisters became closer than ever before knowing we were fighting a common enemy. We laughed and cried together, had deep conversations about life, and called upon the spirits of our parents and grandmother to guide us on our journeys. Besides the use of Western medicine, we felt able to take some control by applying essential oils, administering herbs, and visualizing our cancers disappearing. We now had entered the moment where our healing journey began.

In the beginning of my journey, after I learned of my questionable mortality, I decided at that specific moment that this was not my time to die. I just knew this to be true in the core of my being. I felt it was time to do some research. After I learned about the certainty of my diagnosis, I figured I had something to work with, so I began exploring all of my options in both Western and alternative medicines. I connected with the deepest levels of myself, traveling between the gloomiest as well as the most glorious parts of my soul, both teachers present in my energy field. Then I asked for help from the powers of my mind, emotions, and spirit, requesting that these powers reveal to me visions of a positive healing journey. That's when the spirit of my grandmother showed up in mysterious ways.

What happened next was a powerful transformation of my life, something I never would have experienced had it not been for the diagnosis of cancer.

My Grandmother's Spirit

Years ago, when I attended a Hay House writers' conference, my grandmother's spirit visited me when I was standing in the tiny bathroom of a cruise ship. Her spirit showed me in a vision, the stories of seven of our female ancestors, and told me, "You will write a book about this." So I started the process, and then gave the stories a rest for years, until now. Now that I'd been diagnosed with cancer, my *oma*, the name we call our grandmothers in Holland, came back to support me. And who better could guide me than she who had died of breast cancer herself some forty years ago? "Now it is time to continue and finish what we started," she said. She was also telling me, "When I first gave you the information, it wasn't time to complete the story. It was merely time to plant the seeds in your mind. You first had a lot of living to do before you could weave the threads of the stories of yourself and your ancestors into a tapestry of healing energy, which would then benefit future generations."

She continued to say, "You are sort of a conduit in the middle of two sets of seven generations, the seven past generations and the seven future ones." She also shared that the time we live in is an amazing time of change and discovery. We who are alive today carry in our cellular structure images of who our ancestors were, good and bad. The goal is that by our own demonstrations of healing and letting go of the past, we may help future generations. Therefore, we need to release the imprints of the past generations' experiences stored in the memory cells of our DNA and also release the trials of our present life. The result will be that the next generations will have been purified from old debris and begin a new kind of evolution of humanity. The time has come to drop the old ways of living that no longer serve us.

On Grandmother's visitations, she took me many times on a spiritual journey to a grove of cedar trees, where we met my ancestors who would share their stories. I learned how the unexpressed emotions they had experienced in their lives on earth had left a residue, imprints, in my genetic makeup. With further research I discovered that sometimes we can get sick now, at this present time, because of the imprints of the past, as these can lead to disorders and diseases of the mind and body.

One of the first questions I asked was, "Why me?" Only not in a "poor me" state of mind. I was just curious why this was happening to me. I wondered if there was a connection between my grandmother's cancer and mine, which idea led me to further question the role that my matriarch ancestors played in my life. Their stories became important in my search for generational healing and in my examination of the residue of negative energy stored in the memory cells of my DNA that was possibly contributing to my illness.

Generational Makeup

Of course we also hold in our DNA the energies of our paternal ancestors, but because I had breast cancer and was supported by the spirit of my grandmother who'd also had breast cancer, I decided to explore the matriarch side only. I mainly wanted to focus on the women's stories of the past and of now, given that many of us are now receiving a diagnosis of breast cancer. With the awareness of generational sharing of information came also the important question that, if I carry negative energy in my DNA that maybe leads to illness, how can I heal from that? How can I release that energy from my memory cells?

I was able to look at my parents' humble beginnings, after which I realized how much their life stories, especially their stories of having lived through World War II, were also imprinted in my genetic makeup. Had our family dynamic been created because of that? What I learned from my parents' stories was what a good life I have now, in this amazing time living on earth, and how fortunate my generation is. I appreciate my life even more now that I know how my ancestors have suffered.

Healing can come in many forms. The fact that my sister lost her battle with brain cancer doesn't mean she didn't heal. There was a lot of healing happening in the eighteen months of her journey. One of her greatest achievements was that she had somehow managed to die without having to suffer. I call that prehealing, because she didn't have to lose her independence or her mind. She didn't need to be treated with medicine that could have stretched her life yet would have made her feel miserable—and in the end she would die anyway. I thank God she was spared from that. Healing for her was not to feel the fear or having thoughts of dying without dignity but instead having the freedom to leave her failing body when she could, on her own terms.

In the end, the one thing we can be absolutely certain of is that one day we all will die; no one can escape that fact. What we do with the time in between birth and death, the time that God has granted us, is up to us. We create our lives by what we choose to believe, and we try to discover the mysteries and secrets of who we are and why we are here. In this writing, I try to share the blessings I received along the way of my journey. My wish is that I may be able to consciously leave the most powerful and positive footprints on this earth that I can so as to influence the future for all of my relations.

The information I received will guide me, and hopefully many others, to move through the struggles we face. Our mothers and grandmothers didn't know the effects of the emotions they were dealing with. Carl Jung and Sigmund Freud hadn't discovered yet what happens on the inside when a traumatic event crashes our world. We didn't know how posttraumatic stress disorder (PTSD) would snuff out our lights. Since we have learned so much about why we do the things we do, we now can put all this information to use.

I went back to the knowledge I had learned as an acupuncturist relating to the energy of the meridians located in the body. I also explored other alternatives, like the power of prayer, meditation, and guided imagery, which are used all over the world. I had studied the energy of the life force within essential oils and the laying on of hands, both of which work with the vast field that is surrounding us. Everything in the universe is made up of energy: our thoughts, our emotions, our bodies. The question is, how can we use that energy to our advantage? Throughout my journey, I learned how powerful the mind can be when you talk to the cells and tap into the body's field with the intention of making a difference.

Our Stories

It's time for the women of the world to share their stories. Besides our ancestor's imprints, we have our own experiences to deal with. Each of us has a powerful story to tell about what happened in our lives as children, teenagers, mothers, grandmothers, lovers, and adults. Many have suffered in silence about the ways they were treated and still bury their pain deep down inside. When traumatic experiences are shoved under the rug and silenced, the negative energy builds pressure, like the steam in a pressure cooker. When that hot steam is released, it can cause a crisis that can either lead to a total *breakdown*, where one can fall into a deeper hole, or, if a person seeks help, make way for a *breakthrough*, by releasing the past and leaving it behind, giving the individual a chance to open to her highest potential. There is a fine thread woven throughout the sisterhood of women who share on many levels the same type of emotions no matter where they live in the world, what color their skin is, or what religion they practice. This is the time to band together and give those left behind in the darkness a voice to speak.

Globally

Globally we are in the process of awaking to the light that lives within. When one woman has healed from her old stories, she will touch all other women of the world. Her energy field has changed forever, and her light shines through. We are energetically more connected than we know. Many women who live in other parts of the world are not honored for who they are. Their voices are muffled. Think about the ones who are abused, sold as slaves, receive no education, and/or have no power. How can we make a difference? By healing our own stories, we show the way for others to use their voices. Hopefully we can inspire each other and together support the less fortunate ones. We can keep them in our daily prayers and consciously send them love and compassion. But more than this, we can work on ourselves to heal the parts of us that are wounded, and in so doing find our own positive voices. This will change the energy on a global level.

Sacred Seeds

With the guidance of my grandmother's spirit, I was able to explore the fierce presence of the cancer that had lodged itself in my body like an unwanted guest. By discovering my own power, I was able to let go of this disease and slay the dragon with the strength and courage I gained from those among my ancestors who voiced their experiences in the form of powerful stories.

The healing I received during my cancer journey gave me an appreciation for how precious life is. My core being holds the sacred seeds I share with past and future generations. Those seeds grew into blossoms, showing their beautiful colors that represent all of our voices, freeing us forever.

I feel humbled to have walked this journey with my sister, Coby. I received many blessings from the other side of the veil, and now I realize that life will never be the same. I have come a long way!

Without my grandmother, *Visitors along My Cancer Journey* would never have come to be. Beside my ancestors' input, many other people have walked this journey along with me. A special thank-you goes to my dear friend Pat Nelson who introduced me to the annual writers' conference in Portland Oregon. I'm grateful for Jean Brown who taught me the ropes of writing a story.

Also a warm thank-you, to my wonderful talented coach Maryanne Cohan, who was my greatest cheerleader throughout.

Part I

Part 1

Chapter 1

Guidance On My journey

The Meeting in the Woods

I felt the forest floor under my bare feet with each step I took on this mysterious journey. I thought I recognized the woman who was walking ahead of me and leading the way. I figured she was probably in her midthirties. Her energy felt familiar, yet I didn't know who she was. *This must be a dream,* I thought, but the scenery and the woman accompanying me seemed real, so real that I could smell the fragrance of the tall trees standing along the path, feel the gentle breeze of the wind caressing my hair, and see the unusual but beautiful vibrant colors of nature showing off its glory. I sensed my surroundings communicating with me, giving me a feeling of being protected and safe. The woman walking ahead was dressed in a brown garment with large pockets on each side. Surely her appearance was not of this time. At the waist, a rope held her garment together. Hanging from the rope were bundles of what I suspected to be roots and herbs.

"Keep on following me," she said. "We still have a ways to go before we are at our destination."

"Where are we going?" I asked. "And where am I? Is this a dream or something? I am so confused, feeling that I'm lost here in this nostalgic-looking place where nothing is familiar to me. And I'm getting a little worried. I have this unsettling feeling that I'm up against something I can't explain, something out of the ordinary."

"Don't worry," said the slightly familiar voice, "soon you will learn what this journey is about."

After what seemed like an hour of walking, we entered a small grove of cedar trees standing proudly in support of one another. In the center of the grove, a circle of stones hugged a fire in the middle. The fire pit, in turn, was surrounded by wooden benches to sit on.

"Have a seat, my child," said the mysterious woman in a gentle voice. "This place is a sacred gathering ground for us to meet in. I am the spirit part of your grandmother whom you have been named after. I know you've recognized something familiar in me, but you never knew me at a younger age when I walked on this earthly plane."

I just about fell from the bench. I realized I knew the energy of this woman, my grandmother who had died more than forty years earlier. I had felt her spirit's essence around me in the past, and sometimes, out of the blue, I had received messages in times when I had needed support. How could this be? Why was this experience so confusing? On one hand, I felt I was walking in an ancient, unknown, mysterious forest, and on the other hand, there was something eerily familiar about the whole journey. "What's going on, Oma?" "Why am I here?"

"The reason for you being here has to do with giving our ancestors a voice. I visited you years ago on that cruise ship and revealed information of seven of your female ancestors. But at that time, you had more living to do and had to add the stories of your own journey before you could finish writing. Now it is time to continue.

"The past seven generations of our female ancestors' stories need to be heard, including your life story, which is still evolving, your sister's, your mother's, and mine. In turn, these stories will bring generational healing to your physical, mental, and emotional life, and to the lives of your daughter, your granddaughters, and their offspring for the next seven generations to come of our matriarchal line. Your ancestors' experiences are still stored in the memory cells of your DNA, and it is time to release that which does not serve you. You will be given the names and the stories about the women in more detail in your dreamtime at some point in the future when we all gather together by the fire at the cedar grove."

Oma continued to talk to me, and all of a sudden, I was fading away into a deep abyss between two worlds. I woke up remembering Oma's visit clearly. Then I was pulled back into the reality of my life's latest ordeal.

My sister and I had both been diagnosed with cancer!

A Gloomy Day

It all came crashing down at the wrong time in my life. I was diagnosed with breast cancer. Of course, it is never a good time to hear such bad news, but why now? It had barely been three months since my sister, Coby, was diagnosed with brain cancer. I was still recuperating from the blow of hearing that news. I needed some time to process it all and find the best ways to cope with it. And now I was beginning a journey to a place I had never visited before. Many questions surfaced. The very first one was, Why is this happening to me?

Like my sister and me, many women face the diagnosis of the big C. I knew I was not the only one dealing with this problem, but at that very moment, my focus was on me. I was wondering what it all meant, and figuring out how to walk this journey myself.

Luckily, I was reminded of the fact that many women survive cancer, still after physical treatment they are left with the physical and emotional trauma the disease leaves in its tracks. I consider myself fortunate because I had scheduled a routine mammogram that revealed I had a small lump. From then on, I entered an unknown world and jumped involuntarily on a rollercoaster, taking a journey that led me on a path to the deepest physical, mental, emotional, and spiritual aspects of myself.

As I look back, I am surprised to see that my physical experience of biopsy, surgery, and radiation seemed the easiest for me to deal with. *But how,* I thought, *do I wrap my mind around the fact that something is wrong with me on the inside of my body?* How could I not have known that? The split second after the initial diagnosis, panic crept in, causing me to lose my breath for a moment, and time stood still. I was lost in a dark alley of emptiness, wondering what would happen to me and my loved ones. The next thing I remember was that my logical, thinking mind kicked in and started to ask questions like, What happens if …? I also asked the hows and the whys. The questions, in turn, created fear and anxiety. "Fear of what?" I heard myself asking. *Fear of dying,* was the answer coming from deep inside of me.

I am not ready to do so at this moment, thought my rebellious mind. *It's not my time yet.*

I still have a lot of living to do, said the voice within. *First of all, I want to grow old with my husband and enjoy life to the fullest. I want to witness my kids' journeys in life and support them where I can. And I want to see my grandkids grow up. Besides my family, I have an awesome circle of friends I wouldn't give up for the world. And finally, there is so much I still want to learn and do.* Then I made a pact with myself, affirming I would not die from this disease. I told my husband and kids not to worry. I was 100 percent sure that cancer would not kill me; I knew it in the core of my being.

It's amazing how this crisis dropped me to my knees and led me to reach out to whatever spirit wanted to meet me in my darkest moment. Then, out of the blue, God showed up in the form of the spirit of my Dutch grandmother, paying me a visit from the other side of the veil. Her presence soothed my restless mind. After the emotional shock of the entire experience slightly faded, I could feel her spirit surrounding me like a robe of light. I was delighted by her presence. And I was in need of a mother-like figure, but since my mom had passed years earlier, there was no one who could fill that role to mentor me. Now my sister and I walked this journey together.

I heard the voice of my grandmother say, "You and your sister will be guided throughout this journey; each of you in your own special way will be blessed to meet your ancestors. Remember: you are never alone."

My Cancer Journey

So here I went on my physical journey, starting with biopsy. When the nurse prepped me for the procedure, she asked me how I was doing, and I burst out in tears. I told her about my sister's condition, and all she could say was, "Ah, you poor thing." I know nurses are not trained to deal with people's emotions, but it sure didn't help. After the initial shock of receiving my diagnosis had faded away, I felt deep down inside, for some crazy reason, that I had no cancer. Still, to this day, I'm not sure I had it. But I went through the procedures prescribed for me anyway, and I see the experience as a blessing. The surgery was the first I'd ever had in my life. I have to say that it wasn't bad—especially after my grandmother's spirit paid me a visit that first night, offering her support on my journey, one she had walked herself so many years ago. I was lucky to have been blessed with a high tolerance of pain, so I didn't have to take any medication. Maybe everything went so easily because my tumor was less than a centimeter and I was fortunate not to have been exposed to chemotherapy. Going into Portland every day for my three weeks of radiation, I kept an open mind and visualized the beams of radiation transforming into laser beams and blasting healing energy into my cells. I prayed for the other patients who received radiation and chemotherapy at the same time. I almost felt guilty knowing that the other patients were physically hurting. Why was I so lucky to have such an easy journey? Every day after my treatments, friends would meet me in Vancouver for lunch to support me. It did make a big difference to receive their love and caring energy. On a daily basis, Coby and I shared our journeys, becoming each other's cheerleaders. All the memories I have of my journey are good ones. The only time I detect any residue is when I see or hear something emotional, especially good things. I can cry just like that. I'm not holding on to the memory of being a victim of cancer. I look at it as a blessing, a life teaching that led me on a new path of exploring my existence.

Everything changed after I learned I had cancer. I found myself walking along two paths. One was marked by the harsh truth of a serious, life-threatening diagnosis of cancer for me and my sister, a diagnosis that was toying with our lives. On the other path, I traveled with the spirit of my oma from the other side of the veil, who was adamant she'd be part of my journey. I welcomed her with open arms. But knowing the forbearing lives my parents and grandparents had come from, I felt it was my turn to be strong, fight my battle, and hopefully release the pains of the past and present lurking in my memory cells. All I could do, I thought, was to surrender and walk the uncertain path between these two worlds.

My mother, Gelina de Groot, was born in 1921 in the city of Overschild, Slochteren.

My father, Jacob Looij, was born in 1914, in the city of Den Helder.

Humble Beginnings

My parents married in November of 1939, just before the war started, so I am a child of World War II survivors. Born in 1952, seven years after the war, I was not planned and had come as a surprise. We were poor, but I never knew it. Most people at that time were happy to put food on the table. Fortunately in our house we never felt hungry. I grew up in a family of musicians. For as long I can remember, our house was always filled with music. We would sing together and play the guitar and harmonica. Dad even played the accordion. My first chore started when I was five years old, doing the dishes every night with my big sister. That's when I was introduced to singing. I remember how proud I felt finally to be part of the family's singing tradition. It was as if I had arrived and was not a little girl anymore. My sister would teach me all kinds of songs, in Dutch and English, whatever songs were popular on the radio. My three older siblings were six, eight, and ten years older than me. When I was seven years old a little brother was born. He died at six weeks of age from cancer. A couple of years later my youngest brother was born. I think I had the easiest childhood of all of us—at least that is my impression—but little did I know when I was growing up what a horrible experience my parents had gone through in the five years of World War II.

Meeting My Ancestors

All of a sudden I found myself walking next to Oma on a path in the woods. I could smell the fire from a distance. Soon we arrived at the sacred cedar circle. There around the fire was standing the most beautiful group of women I had ever seen. The love they showed toward me was so peaceful and surreal. Oma took the lead and spoke. "We are gathering here for the first time with the women of your tribe. I have talked to you before about your ancestors, and now I want to introduce all of them so you may get to know them." One by one I was embraced by all the women in the most loving way. I felt honored and blessed to be in their midst and was excited about the opportunity to get to know them better. The last one to approach me was Mom. She looked so beautiful that I hardly recognized her, but I remembered her essence as only a child can recognize her mom. Oma presided in her role as a wise woman. "Let us first pray," she said, "and invite spirit to guide us. Our intent is to offer to the fire the old experiences Gelina endured in her life on earth. In our ceremony we will honor her life and bless her descendants, who still hold the emotional aftermath in their DNA. She will speak her truth about her life experiences living through a war."

Mom's Traumatic War Experience

Mom settled into a beautiful decorated chair with cedar branches, moss, and soft pillows, dedicated for the one to speak. After she was centered, she continued in a soft and clear voice, telling her story. "Life was so different in those days. In the neighborhood where we lived, everyone was poor, but they helped each other out. All changed when the war started in 1940. Our lives took a different course than what we had dreamed of. Not long after, we found ourselves running into bomb shelters whenever we heard the sirens blasting, warning us that airplanes would fly over, possibly dropping bombs. The very first bombing by the Germans in Den Helder was in May 1940. That's when I almost lost my life, only six months into my marriage. While hiding with your dad and many others in a place we thought would be safe, a piece of bomb entered into the chimney of the building and caused an explosion inside. Many people died. One of them was me, so they thought. A peculiar thing happened, for I saw myself watching from above, hovering over my body. It was so serene and peaceful, I felt in no hurry to go back to the chaos down below me, where my body was lying in between other victims. Beside me I noticed other beings floating like me, looking down at their bodies. Some of these spirits drifted up and away, and others tried to get the attention of their loved ones down below. I remember not feeling any fear, any anger, or any other emotion; it was just so peaceful. I witnessed the scenery as a bystander, without any emotion or pain. Next I was pulled into a dark tunnel, seeing light way at the end. When I entered into this twilight zone, a tall being of light took me under his wings and transported me to a place where more light beings resided. There was confusion among the floaters surrounding me. After a while, a nurse-like light being guided me to another light chamber. She spoke to me in a soft angelic voice, telling me I had to go back, for I had more things to accomplish. I felt puzzled. 'I don't want to go back,' I argued. But before I realized it, I floated back into the tunnel. And when I arrived down below, I was hovering again above my body, watching what was happening without emotions or pain.

"When the coast was clear and I guessed that the threat of more bombs dropping had disappeared, people started searching for the wounded and gathering the dead people so their families could claim their bodies. I was able to follow your dad. I screamed at him that I was here, but he didn't hear me. It seemed he was in shock when he learned that I, his beloved wife whom he had stood next to in the shelter, was missing. I saw his body shake to the core of his being. He was in a bewildered state of mind. As he went home, my spirit drifted alongside him, watching him find our home. Then, in a distracted state of mind, he grabbed my picture and, by some means or another, my apron, holding both tight to his heart. He looked so sad and confused when he went searching for me, asking if anyone had seen the woman in the picture he was holding up. There was panic all around; no one had experienced anything like this before. Having noticed a priest walking near him, I tried to get his attention, begging him to go help Dad, but he didn't hear me. Then, like a gift from God, the priest, who knew us through the family, noticed Dad and took him under his wings. 'Come on, Jaap, let's go find her,' he said. After what seemed to be a long time of searching, they found my body lying in the rubble among other wounded and dead people. Looking down at my body, I noticed I was barely breathing. Next I witnessed my limp body being carried to the hospital, where I was placed in the care of nurses and physicians who began fighting for my life. When I felt myself sink back into my physical body, I realized that my injuries were significant, but the most serious injury was on my head. All of a sudden, my body was screaming with pain all over. A gaping wound covered my head, throbbing like a bomb that could explode inside my skull anytime. I was unable to hear

10

anything or respond to the people around me. A nurse gave me a shot in my arm and I lost consciousness again. I faded in and out, but when I came back, I learned they had shaved off all of my hair so as to tend to my wounds. Looking down at my body again, I noticed a scar starting from my forehead and going into my hairline, at least three inches long.

"Because of the accident, I suffered from migraine headaches for the rest of my life. After the accident, my psychic abilities kicked in; I could see things happening before events occurred. Now, in your time, they say that my psychic abilities are the result of a near-death experience (NDE), but at that time, the only thing I remembered was being terrified to share the visions for fear of being ridiculed or, worse, placed in a sanitarium for mentally ill people.

"The war went on. I gave birth to two baby boys in 1941 and 1944. All of us were in survival mode. I was terrified to bring these new lives into the war-ridden world, but I had no choice. I think after the accident I was never the same. I sort of existed, as if life went by me, and did my duties as a wife and mother in a limited capacity, but I never got over the dark days of war. Now they call what I had PTSD (posttraumatic stress disorder).

"War is never, and never will be, a solution to anything. The ones suffering are the innocent people on both sides of the aisle. The German people were just as much victims as the rest of us. Only a handful of people benefit from war. As for me, I have named it already. I had suffered from PTSD, like many of us did. I know now that I died in the war, but I was sent back because I wasn't done yet with my life."

Mom's Psychic Experiences

My mother continued speaking. "I had no control over my psychic experiences; they just happened. I want to share some of them here in the circle, where I feel safe.

"One Sunday afternoon I was lying on the couch trying to sleep off one of my headaches. Your dad was outside in the backyard enjoying the sunshine when the neighbor came home from a soccer game. He, the neighbor, entered into his own backyard, adjacent to ours. After the two men said their normal hellos, the neighbor went inside. All of a sudden I woke up with an eerie feeling, not knowing why. I got up from the couch, walked outside through the backyard, passing your dad, and walked from our yard into the neighbors' without saying a word. I continued on, walking into his home. When I walked into his living room, I was just in time to catch him in my arms. He died instantly, like he'd been waiting for me. Your dad walked in with a curious look on his face, wondering why I had walked into the neighbors' home, people whom we were friendly with but with whom we didn't socialize on a daily basis. After your dad walked in, he took over and called an ambulance. That's when I almost collapsed. Without saying much, I went back home, feeling that I was walking in a haze of confusion. I felt I was in a hypnotic place, not my normal self. There was never an explanation of why I had awakened from my nap with the intuition that someone needed me.

"Another time was on a Saturday evening when Dad and I went to visit friends. At about ten o'clock I had this unsettling feeling that something was wrong at home, but I didn't know what. I knew the kids were home safe with our oldest son, eighteen years old at the time, who was babysitting them with his friend. We rushed home. Upon arriving, we found that everything looked fine. Dad was not happy with me that night, to say the least. The next day I reached for my wallet, which I always placed in a certain spot in the closet but which on this day wasn't there. After searching for a while without any luck finding it, I retraced my steps of the day before, and remembered placing it in the very spot where it always was. The next thing I remembered was the watching eyes of my son's friend following me when I had put the wallet in its place. When I thought back to that incident, I felt an unsettling feeling about the friend for a split second, but I didn't give it much attention. After questioning the lad later that day, we found he had stolen the wallet when your brother had gone upstairs to check on the kids at exactly the time I had felt something was wrong at home the night before.

"These psychic events happened only after my accident in the war, but when they happened, I never questioned whether or not they were real. I just knew. How can you explain such a thing anyway? I would often see shadows of light standing by me, but they only scared me, because I didn't know what they were."

After Mom's powerful sharing, we all sat in silence for a while, sending healing and support to her field of light, blessing her experience. Throughout her telling of her story, I could see the remnants of emotions she'd experienced that dreadful day leaving her field like puffs of dark smoke disappearing, blending into the smoke of the fire. In my own field there was a pulling or tugging motion I could feel, clearing my body. Ribbons of rainbow light moved through the circle, tying us all together as one. We celebrated in meditation for a while, until I felt myself traveling back through the ethers.

Dad and the War

When I was a child, Dad told stories of the war. Almost all of his stories ended well, except for one time. He started telling a story about when he and his buddy were at work and the sirens announced a bomb raid, so they jumped in a ditch to hide. When the bombs dropped, the noise was like a roaring thunderstorm. He went on to tell me and my siblings how the two of them were lying next to each other and all of a sudden his friend got real quiet. That's when Dad realized the person next to him had been hit by a bomb, killing him instantly. He could barely finish the story. He walked away with tears in his eyes, having been triggered by the reminder of that awful moment.

Besides that traumatic day with Mom, my dad had his own scary experiences during the war, but from the moment he learned his beloved wife was still alive, he smothered her with love for the rest of their lives together. Dad was a courageous man who one time stole loaves of bread from a German bread cart. He noticed a little boy standing nearby and gave him a couple of loaves, telling the lad to run home and give them to his mother. When he took some loaves for himself, he was caught by a German soldier, who told him, "If you had not given the boy bread, I would have killed you on the spot." My dad always said that there were many good Germans too, but they had to obey to the rules of war in order to stay alive themselves.

Another time in the Hunger Winter of 1944, Dad, who had to work for the Germans just like other Dutchmen did, found himself smelling delicious fresh-baked fish coming from the Germans' kitchen. Not only that, he also noticed a pile of fish on a plate sitting right inside an open window. He drew close and reached in to steal some. The fish had just come out of the pan of oil. When he grabbed them, they were so hot that he almost burned his hands. He juggled the fish, moving them from one hand to the other, into the air right in front of the kitchen window. The cook, who had seen the whole incident, must have laughed at the sight of fish flying in the air in front of the window. Dad was called in by the German. He thought this would be the end of his life. The German cook, who was a well-respected officer of high rank, told him to sit down at the table. He placed a plate of fish in front of Dad and told him to eat until he was sick. Of course he did eat, thinking this German wanted to have some fun before he killed him. After a while, Dad was released, because the cook didn't want all of his fish to be eaten by this man who had stolen from him in the first place. But just before he left, Dad had the guts to ask the German, "Can I take some fish home for my pregnant wife?" And by golly he got some.

For the rest of his life, Dad would go to Fisherman's Wharf every Saturday to get fish in exchange for other services. He had many fishermen friends who every weekend arrived back home from sea with their weekly catch. They would fill his bag full of fresh fish. With a pile of fish, he went home to clean them and fry them in oil, until he had a pile of fried fish ready to share with others. He would go on his rounds on his bicycle to take fish to his friends and family. He was not a rich man by any means, but he was rich in sharing with others whatever he had. At every visit his friends would give him a beer to drink, so by the time he got home he was pretty funny and ready to eat some fish with his family.

When my elder siblings were old enough, they made breakfast, dusted and vacuumed the house, and cleaned the dishes each day before they went to school. They experienced doing their chores as a normal thing and didn't question why they had to do so much work until they got older. Little did they know that Mom suffered from PTSD and had never recovered from all that had happened to her during the war. She had just stopped living. Her traumatic experiences of the war had snuffed out her beautiful light. The war had shaped her, causing her to live a life of depression that no one understood. It shaped not only her, though; the mental and emotional trauma of the war also shaped Dad, and eventually the entire family, because the emotional experiences imprinted in our parents' genes became part of their kids' makeup as well. My parents' story is part of my story and is linked to the DNA I share with them; it is locked in my memory cells as well. We are all one. The experiences of our parents can leave some residue on our blueprint that, if not cleared, can lead to disease.

The Shift—My Experience

The gift of my sight came from the genetic makeup of my mom. Not until I immigrated to the States in 1980 did I realize I had a touch of my mom's gift of seeing. One of the first times I was conscious of my visions was a year after we had arrived in our new country. Benno, my husband, had his eye on a precious piece of land that was hard to get. One day in July when we were standing at the corner of the land by the boat launch of the Lewis River, dreaming one day the land would be ours, I told him without hesitation that it would be ours in October of that same year. October came and we signed the papers, starting our tulip farm. It felt good to share a part of our old county's heritage in this new land in which we had chosen to live.

My interest in the unknown grew. I started reading books not only to learn about the other world but also to learn more about the English language. In our small town, I found a secondhand bookstore that piqued my interest. When I walked in, I was greeted by a man with a kind face. I asked him if he had any books about UFOs and psychic phenomena. He was kind of busy, he said. He was closing his doors. "Why don't you come back tomorrow? Then I will have some books ready for you." When I came the next day, I saw that he had set aside two boxes of books for me. I bought them for a small price. Back home I found in my treasure boxes many books about what I was interested in and more. The set of books that caught my eye first was the series *Life and Teachings of the Masters of the Far East*, by Baird Spalding. Other books, by Edgar Casey, Ruth Montgomery, Louise Hay and many more authors, led me to develop a deeper interest in the unknown. I was eager to learn this most amazing information available to me. As I studied, I got in touch with my own spirituality and shaped my beliefs. In the next thirty years, new writers came to the surface who studied the connection between science and spirituality in new ways. What I have learned from all these writers is that the evolution of humankind has come a long way.

Many writers talk about the twenty-six-thousand-year period we just finished. The first thirteen thousand years were dominated by the female energy, meaning spirituality, creativity, and caring for others. In the following thirteen thousand years, the male energy influenced the world, with the logical mind, physical strength, and science. One was not better than the other; both were important for our development. The ending of that latter time period was in 2012, causing a shift of consciousness with an opportunity for both male and female energies to blend in each human being.

Now we have crossed the threshold and are entering a new era, one of laying the bridge between science and spirituality. This period has given rise to the study of human DNA and how our genetic makeup affects our lives today. We do research on how PTSD affects the lives of soldiers who have come back from war and how other traumas leave an imprint on our memory cells. With the practice of meditation and other modalities of relaxation, we can tap into our subconscious mind and learn more about the human experience and what the stories of our ancestors are trying to teach us. This new awareness can show us that one of our purposes in life is to have compassion for others, because we are all connected. We are all part of a global journey of a new consciousness.

Chapter 2

My Sister's Cancer Journey

My sister, Coby Looij, was born in 1946, in the city of Den Helder.

Making Plans

One winter morning in 2013, my phone rang. On the other end of the line was the voice of my sister, Coby. "Hi, Sis." She continued in our Dutch language. "I have a plan. What if I come over in the fall and the two of us take a trip together? We haven't done that for a while. Ever since your boys moved away, I've had this dream to visit them and their families in California and Arizona and see how they live. How about it? Oh, and while we are in that area, I want to take you to Bryce Canyon and Zion National Park." I had to laugh. Here she lived six thousand miles away, on the other side of the pond, and wanted to show me these places. She continued saying, "Those places are even more beautiful than the Grand Canyon. So what do you say?"

Of course I wanted to spend time with my one and only sister. It had been fourteen years since just the two of us had gone on a trip to Scotland. We travel well together; spending time together, just the two of us, always brings out the little girls inside us. "Yes," I said, "let's do it." Come to find out, Coby had already looked into airline tickets and possible travel dates, so we were set for our trip about eight months away.

Time flew by. Before I knew it, Coby arrived. This was August of

2013. We first spent time at my home in Washington State, and then a couple of days later we went to Cannon Beach in Oregon with my daughter Nicolette and grandkids Gelina and Harland. Nicolette was thrilled to see her favorite auntie.

When my husband and I immigrated, Nicolette was seven years old, and our sons Ben and Stefan were only four and two, respectively. We realized at that time that the consequences of the move had taken our kids away from their family; we had no one here in the States, except my husband's sister Marion in Pennsylvania, his aunt and her family in Michigan, and my cousin in California, neither one of them living nearby. It was especially hard for our kids not to have grandparents, aunts, uncles, or cousins to grow up around. Because of that, we had a rule of speaking Dutch every night at dinner, so they could still communicate with their grandparents especially, who didn't know any English, in the event that they would come for a visit.

Back from the beach, we hung out a couple of days at home. We took walks along the river and sat out by the pool. Our next trip was traveling with Benno in the RV to Mount Hood for Labor Day weekend. Coby had to laugh at the size of the bus, as she called it. "There is no room for these big vehicles in Europe," she said, "but you crazy Americans know how to bring your entire house with you, and you call it camping!" The weather was just wonderful. We had a great time together, riding bikes in the daytime and sitting outside by the fire at night, talking about the good old days. Of course we had to visit Timberline Lodge. There was still some snow up on the mountain. I feel so fortunate to be living in the beautiful state of Washington, with Oregon nearby.

Coby stayed a couple of more days with us in Washington. We talked about our lives, our parents, and the family we grew up in. Whenever we were alone, we had some deeper discussions about life. Coby told me that her biggest fear of getting older was the prospect of losing her mind like our mother had to Alzheimer's. She even had gone in for a doctor's visit to be checked out because she'd had some dizzy spells now and then. We noticed at times that she was a little absentminded, but aren't we all when we get older?

Family Visits That Sparked Memories of the Old Homeland

Next Coby and I flew to California for our road trip. We rented a car in Santa Barbara that we could drop off at the end of our trip in Saint George, Utah. On our way north to the Central Coast area, we found ourselves driving along the Pacific Ocean with its beautiful coastline. This brought back memories. Our hometown, Den Helder, is surrounded by water on three sides, located by the North Sea and the Wadden Sea. On the west side of town we had sandy beaches, a popular place for tourists. Long ago a sturdy dike was built to protect the land and the city. The country is below sea level. Nowadays we still have the Dutch Navy base and Fisherman's Wharf, where commercial fishing is still one of the biggest industries in town.

At the northwest corner of Den Helder, in a neighborhood called Huisduinen, you can still find the ruins of the settlement Napoleon built when he occupied the Netherlands. It has now been changed into a museum. In 1811 Napoleon visited Den Helder and recognized the importance of building a strategic protective ford. Thus the city became an important marine town. There is so much history in our little town of less than sixty-thousand citizens.

When we grew up, Coby and I would walk the dike in the winter months and watch the ferry to the island Texel come and go. On a clear day you can see the popular island where visitors go and spend a day bike riding. Tourists from afar would spend their vacations there. Another popular thing to do is island-hop. The Dutch Wadden Sea Islands are five jewels to the north of the Netherlands. Each island has its own character, each being quite a bit different to experience. Ferries between the islands make it possible to go and explore them all. You can rent bikes and experience the cute little towns, and also ride through the dunes, where the wind always seems to blow against you.

I remember the weather in the summers being really nice. Whenever we could, Coby and I would go ride our bikes to the beach, lie on the white sand, working on our suntans, and swim in the healing waters of the North Sea. I can still taste the salt water from the sea and feel the sand on my skin. When I first immigrated, I had to go to the ocean at least once a year. It was as if the water called my name like an old friend. Now, I've learned to love the mountains, lakes, and woods of the beautiful Northwest. I've lived longer in the United States than in my native country. Now I feel the local nature running in my blood.

Because Coby and I had arrived late in Santa Barbara, we decided to check into a hotel, thinking the family would probably be asleep already. The following day, we spent time with the California Dobbes. We went biking, on the Bob Jones trail, with daughter in-law Jennifer through the dunes on our way to Avila Beach. We also stopped at a winery, one of many in the area. It almost felt like we were home in the old country, until we arrived at our final destination, the pier of Avila Beach, which extended out into the ocean from the center of town. This little cute village was nothing like our busy hometown.

At night we had dinner with the rest of the family. The kids had just started school about a week before. A couple of years earlier, the family moved from Washington State to California. It took some adjusting for the older girls, but now they love their new surroundings. It wasn't easy when my adult sons moved away with their families. But what can I say? I did the same thing to my parents, even worse. When Benno and I immigrated, my parents thought they would never see us again. Two years later, my parents came for a visit for two months in the summer. How special it was for our kids to have family visiting. I think it enriched all of our lives. My parents would never have visited the States if it hadn't been for us moving here.

Before we left California, Coby went on a tour with my son Ben to see the farm. This was the first time she had visited the family flower farm in Arroyo Grande that we had started in 1986. My husband, Benno, had asked me at that time if I would want to live there instead of on the farm in Woodland, Washington, but I declined because I love the changes of the seasons, which are absent in the Golden State where our farm is located. The main crops growing there are lilies and freesias in our greenhouses. Of course our favorite flowers are the stargazer and Casablanca lilies.

Back on the road again, Cody and I traveled from the Central Coast on our way to visit the Arizona Dobbe family through Los Angeles, with a sleepover in the desert near Palm Springs. The scenery changed from lush green with a view of the ocean to a dry but picturesque desert, each landscape shining in its own glory.

When we approached the Phoenix area, a surprising thunderstorm welcomed us, with rain that lasted for our entire visit with son Stefan and his family. Daughter-in-law Jodi made us feel comfortable. We had a great time with the kids, who were already back at school, and had been for about a month, after the summer break. That night we went to the famous Organ Stop Pizza restaurant, a must-see for visitors. The organ was actually built in 1927 in Denver, Colorado, but was not used much because of the Great Depression of 1930. Later it was almost destroyed in a fire that caused extreme damage to the mechanism. Organ Stop purchased the organ in the early 1970s and rebuilt it into what it is today. In 1975 it was installed in the Mesa, Arizona, location.

Coby, of course, loved the familiar old songs played by the musician. She was standing up and singing along. It was such a treat to see her in her element.

The next day was Saturday, and because the kids had no school, we were able to spend more time with the family. We went bowling. Coby loved to practice her English with the kids. She always noticed the little things about children, the way they shine their light and the funny things they say.

The rain traveled with us when we continued our trip, the weather finally clearing up when we approached our destination, Springdale, by Zion National Park.

Zion National Park was beautiful. The scenery was exquisite. And the weather was finally warming up. The park has some of the most scenic canyons I've ever seen, with spectacular red cliffs carved through the centuries by water. We talked some more, and Coby shared with me that she was quite disoriented at the kids' houses. She didn't know at times which way to go, blaming it on the fact that the houses in the United States are so much bigger than those in Holland, which is true. I noticed she was quiet at times, not herself. I thought she was probably worried about her confusion and her disorientation at unfamiliar places, but deep inside I was worried.

The next day we went to Bryce Canyon. This place carries its own beauty. It felt like I was looking at ancient cities with tall red-colored buildings. What amazing, mind-blowing scenery created by the crimson-colored rock formation. Hoodoos, as they are called, are odd-shaped pillars of rock created by the forces of erosion. It is said that Bryce Canyon has the largest collection of hoodoos in the world. I think Coby made a good point when bragging about this beautiful place. I couldn't make a choice when trying to decide which of the hoodoos was the more spectacular.

I'm very glad my sister took me to these wonderful places. What a treat. Our time together was fabulous, the best we'd ever had. We did a lot of bonding as sisters, growing closer than we'd ever been in our lives. Both of us experienced a renewed sisterhood.

Now the traveling was done and our trip came to an end. We flew back home from Saint George, Utah. It would be two more days before Coby went back to Holland.

My Sister's Shock

A month later I was approached on Facebook by my sister's son-in-law with the news that Coby was in the hospital. What happened was that Coby had been having lunch with a friend who worked at a garage where Coby had her car serviced. They decided to order lunch. When they were eating, Coby's friend noticed something was wrong. When Coby went to take a bite of her sandwich, she would place it next to her mouth. Her friend said, "What's wrong, Coby?" But Coby had no clue what she was doing. The friend took her to the hospital, where she had a seizure. After she was admitted, they did some testing that didn't show any sign of a tumor. So she was sent from Den Helder to Amsterdam, a car ride of a little over an hour, for further testing. Those tests found a cluster of tumors. A brain biopsy concluded what everyone dreaded to hear. Coby indeed had inoperable brain cancer. The doctor said she had only between three months to one year to live.

I felt devastated. My one and only sister was in crisis, and I lived too far away to be near her. How could I ever take care of her, and what would happen next? My first instinct told me to get an airline ticket and fly up there. But what could I do once I was there? I had to wait and see what the course of treatment would be. *What if they are wrong? How could I support her with alternative medicine?* I felt helpless! My mind went on roller-coaster ride, thinking about Cody 24/7. The thought of losing her consumed me. Soon I realized that the only thing I could do was to do research and find anything I could get my hands on to help her, and of course to pray. I asked my prayer circle sisters to pray for her healing in whatever way the spirit would grant to her and for whatever was appropriate and in tune with her soul's wishes.

My mind took me back to the times Cody and I had just spent together. I was wondering if she'd had a premonition in her subconscious mind that something life-changing would happen. You hear it often from other people that they had this big epiphany, a life lesson sent from the realms of spirit, just before they got sick or died. The thought spooked me out. Coby had expressed her concerns when she was here about losing her mind to Alzheimer's. What if God had heard her plea and helped her in providing another way by developing brain cancer? *Hold on,* I thought. *I have to stop thinking like this. This is her journey, and my role is to be there for her in whatever way she needs me to.*

When Coby was recovered from the biopsy, she went through six weeks of radiation in Amsterdam. Five days a week, a cab picked her up in the morning to take her for her radiation appointment, and after she was done the cab took her back home. This was all part of the social insurance of the country. At the same time, the health-care providers gave Coby chemotherapy in pill form. It was administered by mouth and was delivered to her house every night by a nurse. The positive thing was that Coby didn't feel sick at all. Four weeks into the treatment plan, she discovered that the "chemo" pill delivered every day to her house was actually an antinausea pill. No wonder she hadn't gotten sick. Maybe this was part of a greater plan her higher self had arranged for her.

After my research into alternative treatments, I sent Coby curcuma/turmeric supplements to take. I had learned that these help with brain cancer and boost the immune system. I also sent her frankincense essential oil and suggested she place it on the location of her brain stem and on the right side of her head where the tumors were. When she placed the oil on her scalp, she imagined holding an eraser in her hand and erasing all her tumors from her brain with a waving movement.

Whenever I talked to Coby, she was always very positive. She said,

"Well, I just have to go through this. We will see what happens." I never heard her complain about her situation.

Her family and friends set up a system for her so that all she had to do was go to have radiation in Amsterdam and eat whatever meal was brought to her each day. The only setback was that she was a little confused at times. She had talked to her doctor about euthanasia being administered to her if the time were to come when she lost the ability to think for herself. She wanted to die with dignity, something that was very important to her. For years she had seen our mother waste away with Alzheimer's. That was definitely something she was afraid of. So papers were signed indicating that when that terrible time arrived, all they had to do was to get a second doctor's approval for the euthanasia.

One month after the radiation was finished, Coby had an MRI showing that her tumors had shrunk. This was the best news ever, because before radiation they had told her that she would never get better and that the radiation would only prolong her life. Well, they didn't know what the human mind is capable of and especially what my sister is capable of. So now they placed her on another series of chemotherapy, this round for six sessions, each of which was five days on, twenty-eight days off. This was the time when Coby lost her hair and felt a little sick, but not to the extent that she was miserable. At the same time, she still took her curcuma and continued with the frankincense applied to her head. Besides that, she was taking cat's-claw for her immune system.

All in all, Coby's journey, which had looked grim in the beginning, turned into a journey of healing on many levels. She saw that many people cared about her, and she found strength in talking to the spirits of our parents who, she felt, were guiding her. It was sad that she had to stop working. Her private business, providing pedicures and other cosmetology services, was located on the first floor of a building she owned, with her living quarters on the second floor. Now her workspace was vacant and no money was coming in. The only income she had was her pension and the money she received from renting out her garage. But like always, she was a master at managing money. Life went on, and Coby continued to do well with her treatments. We kept in contact on a daily basis, and most of the time she was optimistic.

The Call

Two months after Coby's diagnosis, I was scheduled for a routine mammogram. A couple of days later, I received a phone call to come in for another checkup. I didn't think it was anything serious, because the voice on the other side of the line had reassured me this happens a lot. It was probably nothing. The next thing I learned after this checkup was that I had to go in for a biopsy. One day in January, the day before Benno and I were supposed to leave home to go and visit Coby in Holland, I was called by my primary doctor with the news that they had indeed found a lump. The size of one centimeter, it was cancerous. After the initial shock of the bad news wore off, my thoughts went out to my sister. What would this news do to her psyche? How would I bring it up to her that I had cancer too? Now we were walking together on the same kind of journey. I would face her in less than twenty-four hours and was wondering how to share the bad news with her.

Sharing the Journey

Soon after I arrived in Holland and settled in with Coby, I shared the news of my cancer diagnosis with her. I reassured her that I would be fine. This small lump would not get me down, and I was sure it wouldn't take my life. I had the best example, learning from her, of how to deal with a serious diagnosis like cancer.

It was nice to witness the support she received. Every morning, afternoon, and night she would be visited by friends and family, and she loved it. Everyone in return loved to spend time with her. I noticed that many would come to her with their problems, which showed the role she played in other people's lives. Through the course of her cancer journey, she stayed positive. And she kept on finding strength in her belief that our parents' spirits were guiding her.

One night, after the visitors had left, Coby and I were having a deep conversation about our mom and dad. Every night Coby placed a candle in front of our parents' picture, which stood atop her computer cabinet. From that vantage point, they were able to overlook the entire room. Because of her nightly ritual, I felt that our parents were watching over us, sending their love and support. Coby would ask them for prayers of healing every day. During the daytime, a pair of doves showed up on her balcony. Coby would feed them, calling them by the names of our parents. She could see the character of our parents in those birds, noticing how the male protected the female, like our dad used to do with Mom, chasing away the other birds that were trying to steal their food. We were in deep conversation about our lives, our diagnoses of cancer, and of course our parents, when out of the blue music started to play! The whole room was filled with the sweet sound of instrumental music. We both stood up, looking as if we were nailed to the floor, with chills running down our backs and goose bumps on our arms. We looked around trying to find where the music was coming from. Then we discovered that the sound was coming from Coby's computer while it was turned off. As a matter of fact, everything was turned off, the radio, the TV, and the computer. We were perplexed, not knowing what to think at first. Then we both knew in an instant that it was our parents who had taken the opportunity to say hi through the energy of music, an important medium in our family. When we came to our senses, we both said out loud, "Thanks, Mom and Dad. We know you are here." The music stopped. "What the heck just happened! Oh my gosh, we were visited by the spirits of our parents." It was a thrill that is hard to describe. Who would have thought three months ago that we would see each other so soon and share our cancer journeys with the support of our parents' spirits?

Because Coby was older, we didn't play together much as children, but we became very close when I was in my teens, and even closer when we both had kids. I guess she cleared the way for me. Younger siblings often have it easier growing up. She started singing in a band with our oldest brother when she was only sixteen years old. They played for thirty years together. She loved that lifestyle and didn't mind being on stage. I, on the other hand, was more of a homebody. I felt different from everyone else in my family. I often thought I had been delivered to the wrong family, but it turned out that it was the best family, as God had picked it out for me. In my family of origin is where I learned some major life lessons, especially about how music can heal.

Chapter 3

A Last Farewell

Crossing Over on the Wings of the Seagull

On the first day of May 2015, my friend Julie and I sat outside on her deck enjoying the nice spring sunshine. The next day, Saturday, we would be teaching our monthly class titled Woman of Spirit. On this morning we were getting together to prepare the outline of what we would be teaching tomorrow. Suddenly the sound of a car driving onto her private road disrupted our conversation. "What idiot drives so fast on my road?" asked Julie. After a couple of minutes, we learned that the driver was my husband, Benno, who walked up to us with a sad expression on his face. I felt this unsettled feeling, like a rock in my stomach, telling me that something was very wrong. I was soon to find out what. He brought the disturbing news that my sister, Coby, was in a coma after having suffered a seizure the previous night. They had found her some twenty hours later and rushed her to hospice. My body went numb; my mind was perplexed. When Benno and I sat down trying to figure out if we would go to Holland or not, my phone rang. On the other end of the line was the voice of my daughter Nicolette, who was back home working at the family farm. She was difficult to understand because of the weak phone connection at Julie's place. I told her that we knew about Coby being in a coma. I said that I hoped she could hear me well enough and could understand that we would be coming home soon. The connection broke off, so Benno and I decided to leave, both of us with an unsettled feeling of not really knowing what was going on. When we arrived home twenty minutes later, we learned that Coby had crossed over peacefully in the presence of her adopted son Roel, his wife Karin, and Coby's best friends Mandy and Sjaak.

All of a sudden I found myself in a strange place. I recognized the reality that my sister was gone, yet I did not understand any of it. It was almost like being in two worlds at once, neither of them clear. It didn't sink in that I would never see her again, or that never again would we laugh together until we peed our pants, or that never again would we have deep conversations about life. Her presence was gone. I already started to feel the void her passing had created in my energy field. I was thinking how strange it is when someone leaves your life, either by death or separation. The vibration of my energy field was off. I knew I would never be the same; of that I was sure. A part of me was missing. I knew that it takes time to fill such a void, knowing it will never be the same no matter whom or what it is replaced with. Although I felt sad that Coby was gone, I was also very happy for her that her wish was fulfilled. Her biggest fear was that the tumors in her brain would cause her to lose her mind and become dependent on others. Thank God she had been spared from that. No one wants that for their loved ones. I knew she was in a good place now, healthy and happy. The hard thing was that the ones left behind felt the grief of her not being there anymore, but she was just fine, without worries, bills to pay, or people to please.

The next day I received a gift while teaching the class with Julie. We have a wonderful group of women we work with, and we always say that we are all teachers and students of each other, which is true. I received a lot of support that day after I shared about my sister's passing. Coby's death became part of the teaching that day, about how the loss of a loved one affects us. In the afternoon we did an exercise outdoors, connecting with the energy of trees and asking nature to teach us the lessons each of us needed to learn in our own way. When I was standing by a birch tree, I felt the support of energy embrace me. When I connected with the energy of the tree, I noticed the bark of the tree peeling away, as if it was letting go. I gathered the peeled bark. When I looked closely, I saw that it looked like paper with lines of words written on it. I instantly knew this meant that I must finish the last chapter of my book. The time had come for me to reflect on Coby's life, as well as mine, and start writing it all down. *How clever of spirit to show me this synchronicity,* I thought. Then I heard a voice say, "Why do you think the writing of this book was on hold? Because you two had to live through the journey and finish this chapter of your lives together. Your sister and you will be forever part of each other's cancer journey." I knew this was a great opportunity to heal and to process Coby's passing.

Deep down inside, I had known that the moment of her passing would come, but it was still unexpected when it happened. It still had caught me off guard. I was not ready to hear that news. When Coby was diagnosed with her brain cancer, they gave her three months to a year to live. How Western medical doctors have the audacity to play God with their diagnoses is beyond me. No one knows when it's your time to go. I've seen people buy into this type of practice and, through their beliefs, trust in their doctors. Many of these people died almost to the day it had been predicted they would. Anyway, Coby lived on for eighteen months after her diagnosis, in full consciousness. It was a blessing that she'd never felt really sick like some people do. She had just received news from her doctor a month prior that she could fly again and was making plans to come for a visit to the United States in the summer. *What a gift,* I thought, *that she died with that dream on her mind.* I was actually happy for her that she had gone at a time when she still felt good. She was surrounded by people who loved and supported her.

A couple of hours later, Benno and I had purchased tickets to fly to Holland with our daughter Nicolette for Coby's service. It is a strange experience when one of your loved ones dies. It's hard to wrap your mind around the fact that you will never see them again. It takes time to sink in. *What, all of a sudden I can't pick up the phone and call her anymore? I guess I can talk to her directly now. I hope she is available; she might be too busy doing other things, you know!* At night my mind flooded with memories. I remembered her laugh and the way she spoke. I often heard her saying, "They say I'm sick, but I don't feel sick. They must be talking about someone else." She enjoyed the large number of people who visited her every day, and she was always in awe that so many came. I told her that she had created that herself, because she was a pleasure to visit with and would never complain about her situation. She always had nice conversation to share. She knew many people, and many knew her. Whenever I was home for a visit and she and I would go out into town, there was always someone who recognized her, either from the time she was a singer for thirty years, or from when she owned a bar for a couple of years, or from her work as a pedicurist. I always said jokingly, "It feels like the paparazzi are following you wherever you go."

I started to contemplate what to say about Coby's life and singing career in her eulogy. Because most people knew her through her music, I decided to show another side of who she was. The night before her service, I asked her spirit if she had something to add. I told her about my plan to talk about the "imprint" she had left behind. I could hear her respond in my mind. *We could give a gift to everyone present by reminding everybody that we all have ways to leave imprints, and we can uplift others by the positive imprints we leave behind,* she said.

Perfect, I thought. *What a way to leave a last imprint, with such a powerful message.*

The Celebration of Her Life

Coby and I grew up being the only two girls in a family of five. One of my first memories was doing dishes with my sister every night, starting from when I was five years old. She was washing; I was drying. While doing our chores, we would sing the latest melodies of the Top 40. I considered myself lucky to be in a family with two older teenage brothers and my sister who was approaching her teenage years. All of us loved music, including our parents. Because we were poor, there was no money to send the boys for guitar lessons, but that didn't stop them from learning. My oldest brother would sit on the stairs strumming and practicing his guitar for hours along with the radio whenever he had a chance, until he figured out how to play a song. Of course we didn't have TV at that time to watch shows; all we had was the radio, which we would allow us to listen to music or a play. I remember vividly when my big sister taught me my first English song, which we would sing at night in the kitchen. The song was "Let It Be Me," by the Everly Brothers. Despite having learned the lyrics, I had no clue what the song was about. Our native language was Dutch, not in any way close to the language of the songs I was learning, but somehow I picked up the meaning pretty fast.

So on my talk at Coby's memorial, I started out by recalling how she had affected my life with her music. I mentioned that it was our chore to do the dishes every night and that while doing so we would sing with the kitchen window open, the windows having fogged up from the heat of the cooking. What we didn't know was that the neighbors were listening to us singing every night. We lived in a row house in a neighborhood where all the kitchens and backyards were connected, so it was easy for the neighbors to hear us. The melancholic memory of us singing in the kitchen took me back in time. I heard us sing, "I bless the day I found you. I want to stay around you." Coby's love of singing lives forth in her daughter and granddaughter. Her positive outlook during her illness and her curiosity to learn also left a large imprint.

Then I told the story not many people knew about her, the story of the seagull pecking on her kitchen window the day after our dad died in 2003. The seagull and Coby became friends. She found in him an ally that came to visit every day. She called him Jaapie, after our dad, whose name was Jaap (Jacob). The seagull gave her comfort, as good companions do. A year later our mother died. When we left the funeral home after Mom's service that day, the seagull flew over. Coby pointed at the bird and elbowed me, saying, "Look, there is Jaapie. He is here to pick up Mother Lientje." She said it as a matter of fact, like it was a normal thing, something to be expected. In the days following Mom's service, the seagull no longer showed himself. Coby accepted the fact that our parents were together now and in a better place. I also told those who had gathered for Coby's memorial all about the pair of doves showing up.

The service was beautiful, a well-deserved farewell. Recordings of Coby's voice singing "The Rose" and "Hero," initially performed by Bette Midler, were played between the speeches of those who paid their last respects. Benno was the final one to talk. He told beautiful stories of things we had experienced over the years. All in all, Coby's life was celebrated with love and light. Then something odd happened. The minute Benno sat down, a seagull landed on the skylight above us, scratching the glass like it wanted to come into the auditorium. It squealed a loud sound that almost blended in with the music. Everyone heard it. If it hadn't been for my story, I'm sure it would have gone unnoticed. Coby said her last farewell and sang her last song. Music was her life, and she made sure that her last note was heard by all. She left on a high note and flew into the distance.

It was comforting to learn that Coby had been treated with respect at the hospice place. While she was there for only a couple of hours, when it was time for her casket to be carried out, all the employees stood outside, lining the way and showing respect. The same procession unfolded when her casket was carried out from the auditorium to the car that would be taking her to the crematorium. We all walked next to her casket saying our last goodbyes.

The world had been blessed with Coby's presence. For me, I was blessed to have had such a wonderful sister. But most of all I feel blessed to have shared this cancer journey with her and learned how strong she was.

Now the seagull is gone, and the doves have not been spotted either. All that is left to say is, You will be missed by many, my dear sister. Yours was a life well lived. I love you forever. We will see you on the other side.

Chapter 4

Family Dynamics

Oh, Brother

One year after Coby's death, Benno and I were about to take our entire family to Holland to connect with our roots. Benno had been planning this trip for a couple of years now. The grandkids were looking forward to learning more about where their parents were born and to meeting their Dutch relatives. One day of our itinerary was dedicated to going to my hometown and introducing my American family to my Dutch family and friends. We had planned to have lunch with my brothers and their families, having invited them months prior to the event. About five weeks before our trip, I received an email from my youngest brother, Ron, stating that he and his wife, Hannie, didn't want to join us for lunch because of all that had happened between my brothers and sister in the past. They felt we had chosen my sister's side.

Shocked to hear the news, I had to process the accusation leveled against me. What had happened between my siblings was none of my business, I thought. I was wondering what my role was in this messed-up family feud. Had I even played a role in it, and if so, how? I went back in my mind to one year ago, remembering that none of my brothers were present at Coby's funeral. After the service, we went to visit all of them, but not a word was said about her passing. I knew their relationships were not up to par and thought it not my place to interfere. For me the emotions of losing my sister were still raw. Now, one year later, I was accused of choosing sides, and because of that my youngest brother and his wife were not interested in meeting my family. I recalled a similar experience some twenty years ago. Obviously my sister had spread the word that I had called my brothers a certain name. But when they revealed to me what she had said, I realized I didn't even know that name, so how could I have said such a thing? That's how a false impression of me had been created. I wasn't aware of any of it. I wondered what else had been said about me that had created a rift between my brothers and me. I guess I will never know. But to come back to what I was accused of, I would have to say, no, I hadn't chosen sides, and yes, I was guilty of spending more time with my sister, but she was also more interested in me than my brothers were. What a mess. I went over the email again and again, crying and praying about what to do. Finally I came up with a plan to meet with my brother and his wife to talk things out, so I emailed him back to see if that would work for them. It did. This was big for both of us, since we had never learned how to communicate in our family. Instead, things would hang in the air forever and would never be resolved. We all worked out our emotions in our heads and spun them in such a way that they would turn into a big drama in our minds, leading to hurt feelings and emotional shutdown. We are all guilty of that, and it is how we created the karma between us. This time I was willing to do some damage control with an open mind. Benno and I scheduled to see Ron and Hannie the day after our arrival in Holland. It was not the start of our family vacation I had pictured, but maybe it was the start of a new understanding between my brother and me.

Contemplating the Meeting

After a ten-hour flight, we arrived in Amsterdam. We were a week ahead of the rest of the family for the vacation we hoped would be the trip of a lifetime. Tired from having skipped a night's sleep, we decided to take a nap after arriving at our hotel. Later that night I had a hard time falling asleep, maybe because of my jet lag or the earlier nap that afternoon. Or could it be I was worried about meeting my brother and his wife the next day? I was tossing and turning all night, trying to find the right words to say in the morning. Earlier, Benno had asked me what I was going to say at the meeting. I didn't know for sure. But in the wee hours of that morning, when I was lying awake, not able to sleep, the spirit of Mom joined my mind.

Mom Teaching Family Dynamics From Beyond

"What's troubling you, my daughter?" I heard a voice say in the distance of my mind. I felt jolted into space and realized I was once again at the sacred circle with the women of my tribe. The crackling fire felt nice and cozy, and in an instant I felt safe and at home with my beautiful ancestors on the other side of the veil. To my pleasant surprise, Coby was present for the first time at the circle. "Your sister's spirit is here, present in silence," said the voice, "because she is still processing her life experiences." After I adjusted to my surroundings, the voice belonging to the one now sitting next to me asked the same question again, when I realized this voice was my mom's. I felt unconditionally loved by her spirit at that moment. With beauty and light radiating from her presence, she looked different in the realm of the spiritual world. I was happy to see that she was free of her past trials. There was no residue from the trauma she'd endured.

"Every emotion we experienced on earth begins to clear as soon as we arrive on the side. After the cleansing, only the stories are left. No trauma or emotion affects us anymore, unlike what you are feeling now," my mother said. She must have watched me struggling with the unsettling message I'd received from my younger brother. I wondered if the drama between her children here on earth still affected her on the other side in some way. "Tell us your story today," she said in a gentle voice, "for telling your story will help you heal and will clear your memory cells." So I shared my part of the story and said that I felt hurt about having been drawn into the family drama, knowing I had not been present when all their issues developed but still being blamed for allegedly having chosen sides. What was my part in this drama? I wanted to know."

Purpose and Lessons

"Let's look at the drama from a different angle," continued Mom's voice. "Imagine that before we are born we sit in council together with our family-to-be, dividing the roles we are to play in each other's lives. What if you have chosen your parents, siblings, spouse, and children to learn certain lessons? How would that serve you, and what would be the purpose of it? Think about the fact that the stories circulating in the family are in tune with each member's soul's wish to learn and grow. Maybe the soul group decided to learn lessons in order to let go of karma. This karma is created when souls play out the same scenarios over and over again without resolving anything. These stories leave a negative film in our physical field while we are on earth, and the negative fields can stay with us from lifetime to lifetime, until we release them. Through awareness we can transform the old ways and learn to have compassion for each other, freeing each other from the old contracts agreed upon. Because the new wave of energy entered the world in the year 2012, we now have an opportunity to resolve karma. What if that is the purpose of your all being there together on earth? The only way to learn together is to dive into the family dynamics and change how we respond to each other's drama. If only one member of the soul group drops their karma with compassion, they set free the vibration of the entire soul group, leading to a change in the vibration of the entire world. These are the lessons and the purpose of the soul group."

Family Roles

My mother continued speaking. "The purpose of playing the different role is to learn from each other and be each other's teachers. It's how we help each other out. One will be the victim, the one who carries the negativity of the entire family. Another may play the role of the clown, bringing some laughter at times of difficulty, and yet another will play the role of peacemaker, the one who brings calming energy to aggressive situations. Yet another role is that of scapegoat, the one who takes the blame for everything so that everyone else can dump their problems on them. Still another can be a hero or a savior. In the dynamics of the family, members play out their roles like actors performing a dramatic plot. The one who is giving you the most heartache is many times your greatest teacher, but of course people will hardly ever recognize that or even want to acknowledge it. We only focus on the pain they have caused us." She continued to reveal the roles played out in our family, which information I was to share with my brother and his wife the next day.

"Now I have a question for you, Mom. How did you process the things that happened to you in the war? Were you angry with the Germans? What were the roles you and Dad played in our family? Did you have any inkling how the war had affected your family life and your relationships with others?"

"You might say I was bitter about what happened to me in the war and about the suffering I had to endure throughout my life with headaches as a result of the bombing accident. What we didn't know at that time was the effect the war had on all of us on an emotional level. One of our purposes was to show the world how a war damages innocent lives. After a while we became numb. Our escape was to gather together in song, dance, and acting, and whenever we could we would drink away our pain.

"Earlier you wondered if the family dramas created on earth still affect us on this side of the veil. My answer is that we are not emotionally involved with earthly dramas. The only emotion we know here is love. You will learn that by watching us here at the circle by the cedar grove. We are not dwelling on the experiences we had in our past lives. For us, our past life turns into a story. Only the people who are in the physical on earth are experiencing the emotions stored in the memory cells of their body. We are just fine here on the other side. It is our hope that we can guide you all and help you clean up the debris of past generations stored in your physical DNA. This will help the future generations to start with a clean slate. From this side we can see how the roles we chose to play in our life affected the family dynamics. Soon after we die, we visit the life just lived and learn about the mistakes we made and the effect those mistakes had on others. Then we are cleansed of the emotions experienced in that life, and all that's left is our story. After our review, our story, together with other past life experiences we had, will be recorded in the library called the Akashic records. As spiritual beings, we continue to learn and grow, hoping to get the opportunity to guide our soul groups still living out the dramas on earth.

"We in spirit and you on earth are all connected. We merely exist in a different form. That is the reason we guide our loved ones. Many are open to and aware of spirits around them. All we can do is pray humankind is willing to receive our love and guidance. Like with you, you opened up to your grandmother's call, as do many people nowadays who feel connected with the spirits of their ancestors. This is all part of this new shift happening on earth. Many people are waking up. This awakening will help change the vibration of humanity and of the earth, leading to a new wave of positive energy being exposed. But for now, you have enough information to share with your brother and his wife. When you share this story with them, I know they will feel it on a deep level."

It was very helpful to be emotionally removed from the family trauma for a moment and look at the issues at hand from a different angle. This gave me courage to face my brother and his wife later that morning. In my mind I created a picture of how the conversation would play out, assuming that things always work out differently from how you imagined them. So all I could do was to surrender, knowing my mom's spirit was right there beside me. In the wee hours of the morning, I drifted off into a restful sleep.

The Meeting of the Minds

Our drive to my hometown seemed to take forever, but we finally arrived at my brother's home. After the normal greetings, I decided to dive right in by saying, "Let's put it all on the table. Why are we here?" The conversation started with Ron and Hannie explaining how they felt about me not having visited them whenever I came to stay with my sister, who lived just around the corner. They had a good point there. I totally understood where they were coming from. All I could do was agree that that was wrong of me. I couldn't, however, change it. The damage was done, and I was at fault. What I did say was that I had only one sister and that she and I were really close. My brothers, on the other hand, had their own close relationships. I think that's normal. Not all siblings get along equally.

Another reason why Benno and I had failed to visit Ron and Hannie was an incident that had happened a couple of years prior when we paid them a visit. While we were at their house, my brother's best friend dropped in. Just a week before, this friend had sent Benno a nasty letter not related to my brother. We wrongfully assumed that my brother and his friend had talked behind our backs about the letter, so we felt very uncomfortable. When I brought it up, Ron said that he had no knowledge of his friend writing the letter. I believed him. I had been wrong in assuming. So you see how my false assumption created a rift between us. I had twisted the story in a dramatic way, whereas he didn't know anything about the situation.

When I immigrated to the United States, my sister was the one writing and calling me, and she came visit me many times. She also invited me to stay with her whenever I would come for a visit. None of my brothers ever invited us for dinner or even just a visit. It was not common in our family to do so; you just drop in.

All three of my brothers connected better with my husband than with me. I always felt they had no interest in me, a leftover from my childhood, where I was not noticed. Even the emails they wrote were sent to Benno.

So the conversation with my brother and his wife went back and forth, with each of us sort of blaming the other. After all, I had been accused of choosing my sister's side. There was also an attempt to talk about Coby. My brother believed she acted as if she were his mother and said that she was very hard on his now wife. The hatred that Ron and Hannie felt for Coby was palpable. They knew I didn't want to hear about it. She had been gone for only a year. I wondered why they were so angry with her. Since they hadn't spoken in years, could it be that they had heard others speak badly about her and misrepresent her story? I didn't want to be dragged into the family drama I had not been part of. It all happened between my brothers and our sister. What is sad about their feelings toward Coby is that she has no knowledge of what they think of her. They are the ones keeping that image of her alive in a hateful way, and sadly it hurts only them.

Mom's Family Dynamics Explained

At one point in the conversation I remembered what my mom had told me in the wee hours of that morning. I told my brother and his wife that I had a story to tell about our family dynamics. I continued talking about how our parents' lives had started, beginning with their marriage, just before the war, and then Mom's accident. I mentioned how Dad, from that moment on, adored his wife and did everything to please her. What followed in their lives was the birth of the two oldest brothers, both born as the war raged on. Can you imagine being that woman in the story having to go through all that trauma? When I told the story, I suggested that we look from the sidelines and be a witness only, feeling no emotion or pain.

"So here starts the family dynamics," I continued, "of this wounded family who are doing their best with the tools they have. No one knew at that time the effects war has on a person, probably because most people around them were dealing with the same things. Everyone was just in survival mode. That's all they could handle. So life went on, and Mom was checked out most of the time because of her PTSD and headaches. All she could do was take care of her family as best she could. The kids got older and went to school; no one noticed Mom's depression and low energy. Now, the kids helped her out in the morning by making breakfast, doing the dishes, dusting, etc., before they went to school. The family dynamics seemed to work well, each of us playing our assigned roles."

The Roles We Played in Our Family

I clearly remembered Mom's input about the roles played in our family, so I started to tell Ron and Hannie what I had learned.

The oldest brother played the role of victim. He was conceived at a time when Mom was still recovering from her accident. When he was born, his light was overshadowed by all the fear of those around him. The heavy energy of the war was imprinted in his field, so he became as much a victim as the others who lived in his immediate surroundings. In a way he lightened their load by helping them carry theirs. How could he not? Now in his seventies, he is still playing music for senior citizens, bringing joy to their lives, making them forget their struggles for a moment.

The second child born in the last year of the war didn't feel the heaviness in his field. He took on the role of the clown, making everyone laugh, bringing smiles to their faces, and breaking the intense moments of pain and suffering. Although the heaviness and fear were palpable in the fields of those surrounding him, he somehow found a way not to be affected by their energy. Instead, he lightened their heavy energy of victimhood a little at a time. This much needed laughter cleared their fields of darkness somewhat.

Third in line was our sister, Coby, who played the role of the scapegoat. She took over many of Mom's jobs. Even so, no one noticed her hard work. Whenever something went wrong in the household, she was blamed for it. She was fourteen years old when Ron was born, already working a full-time job at a factory. When she came home at night, she first had to do the dishes with me after dinner, and then take care of Ron, the baby, feeding him, bathing him, and putting him to bed. She played the role of being Ron's mom for at least two years, her role as Cinderella. She came into the world at a time after the war when everyone was still healing from their horrible experiences and, at the same time, learning to celebrate their newfound freedom. In their processing of mental and emotional traumas, they needed a scapegoat to dump their darkness on, so that's the role Coby's spirit chose to play. That's how she became the Cinderella of the family.

The fourth child in line was me, the second girl. My spirit had decided to play the role of peacemaker. Life passed me by because I was living in an alternative world of fantasy, finding solace in silence. God must have had a plan to send me down the chute because the tribe hadn't planned on another family member disturbing their so-called "peace." Here I came, a mistake, but a new thing to focus on, for all to love, helping them to set aside their problems. This new baby turned out to be calm and loving—just what Mom needed. I was the lost child; no one noticed I was there. And so I started my role as the peacemaker, staying quiet most of the time.

The fifth child only stayed for a short time. His role was to help Mom to open her closed-off heart and to show her that life could be precious. I was not yet six years old when my baby brother was born. I remember how excited I was to have a little brother. Unfortunately he died from an abdominal mass at only six weeks old. He came in to help Mom work through her depression. She was devastated when he died. After all of the trauma she had suffered in her life, she couldn't handle another disaster. She was done. And that's when her mother and twin sister noticed she didn't want to live anymore. Just imagine what she had already been through in her life, and now this. It was just too much! Dad didn't know what to do. In despair he went to consult the doctor, who advised to have another baby.

So, a year later, Ron was the sixth child born. Here came this child who was the hero, who literally saved Mom's life. Her heart was open again and she had a new perspective on life. She adored her son and put all of her love in him, so much so that Dad became very jealous of this baby boy. What about Dad now? It took him back to his own childhood, living in a large family, not being noticed, always competing for his mother's love. Ron chose the lesson of discovering his place between dark and light, love and hate, finding his voice and being a beacon of brightness for others.

Dad coped with life by working day and night. He was a deeply wounded man with limited skills to express himself. I hardly ever saw him, only for dinner, and then he was off again to work a side job. And Mom just looked good on the outside. No one knew what went on in that head of hers. So that's how the family dynamics were created.

I purposely left out the fact of the gathering of our souls before birth, not knowing if this would be too spooky for Ron and Hannie.

I was kind of surprised by how intently they had listened to me tell the story. That was the first time I'd ever felt I had the attention of a family member besides my sister. I wanted to bring home the fact that through the roles we play in a family and how we interact with each other, the words spoken from one member to another often get distorted. In the family unit we interpret and spin our stories in such a way that they fit in with our own beliefs. Many times we change the context of what we heard from others, so the truth of the story gets lost. That's how family feuds start, by people assuming words were said that were not said. To make my point even clearer, I gave the example of a group of children sitting in circle, with one whispering a message to the next one and then the next. When the last child reveals the final interpretation of the words, the group discovers how different the message is from when it started.

I'd felt empowered to tell the story as well as I could. I'd finally found my voice to express myself. My only hope was that Ron and Hannie would get something out of it and heal the hatred they felt in their hearts toward my sister, and maybe even explore where the stories about her originated. Now the ball was in their court. All I could hope for was that they would come meet my family in two weeks. If not, I would understand and forgive them, not taking it personally, because whatever happened would be a reflection of where they were at that moment in time in their lives.

Two weeks went by fast. Benno and I showed our American family the history of our country, Holland. To my surprise, one of the kids' favorite visits was to the Anne Frank House. Most of them had read the book *The Diary of a Young Girl* in school, and it had made a great impression on them. On the day of my hometown visit, I was delighted when all three of my brothers showed up for lunch with their families. I give my youngest brother and his wife all the credit for finding the courage to speak up and express what was on their mind, a luxury we hadn't had growing up. I felt proud to show off my American family, and equally proud to introduce my Dutch family to the grandkids, who as a result were exposed to the Dutch roots of their bloodline and the branch of DNA they share with their parents and grandparents.

Chapter 5

My Oma's Story

My oma was born Klazina Wilhelmina Niewold in 1899, in Sappemeer/
Slochteren.

My Memories of My Oma

One of the fondest memories I have of my oma is of something that
happened when I was seven years old. That summer I got to spend an
entire week at my grandparents' house. During the day it was just Oma
and me while Opa (Grandfather) was at work. For me, in my little girl's
mind, it was a big vacation away from home. It didn't matter that it
was only one block away. I had heard other kids tell stories about going
away on vacation to magical places that captured my imagination, and
I'd always felt left out until this time. Now I also had a story to tell.
It was the first time in my life being away from home all by myself.
I realize now the reason why my grandparents took me in. It was to
relieve my mother, who was grieving the loss of her son. Anyway,
with no knowledge of that, I felt lucky to spend time with my oma. In
the morning we would feed the chickens, collect the eggs, and cook
the latter for breakfast. We would make the most delicious soup from
fresh-picked vegetables from her garden and little rolled meatballs for
extra flavor. Ever since that day, I have never tasted any soup that even
comes close to the one she made.

At night I would sleep on the guest bed, on a mattress filled with real straw. When I awoke in the morning, I found myself sunken in the middle of the mattress. The straw had flattened underneath me. The house my grandparents lived in was so little that it didn't have an indoor bathroom. But even so, I was fascinated by the outhouse, two steps away from the kitchen's back door. During the day we would play games, practice writing, and walk to the store just around the corner, like Oma did every day, to get what was needed for the daily meals. I enjoyed every minute of the attention I received from Oma during the time she and I spent together.

On Sundays we children went to Oma's house with our parents, and many times she made my favorite vegetable soup. The entire family got together, and the adults would play card games. Cigarette smoke filled the little house, with everyone smoking. On top of that, Opa added flavor to the thick air, because he was smoking cigars. I also remember the little shot glasses of alcohol they would sip on. Unfortunately for me, I was the only child of the family of my age, so I had no one to play with. I would find other kids who lived nearby in the neighborhood.

Oma was a quiet person, much like me. My family was not affectionate. I don't remember ever sitting on Mom's or Oma's lap or ever being told they loved me. They just didn't do that. But I knew no different, so I wasn't traumatized by it. It was just the way it was. I knew that I was loved. When I think back to the time when I was between five and ten years old, I feel the gloomy family energy. There was a heaviness in the air that I couldn't explain in my young mind. Of course I didn't know anything about the trauma they'd all experienced in the war, like the fact that the husband of one of my aunts had died, leaving her with a daughter to raise by herself. Another aunt's husband, who was a trader in the war, left her to raise her son by herself. On top of that, there was Mom's accident—and then the fear that everyone had gone through. The time of war had wounded them all severely. All they could do was make the best out of life.

Oma (Klazina) was born in 1899 in the town of Slochteren, in the province of Groningen, in the country of the Netherlands. She was the next to the youngest in a family of eight children. Her father was a land worker; he worked in the fields of the surrounding agricultural farms. He died when she was only two years old. As a child, she was very sensitive to the feelings of others and knew that something was wrong the minute a suffering person walked in through the door. We now call that being empathic. When she was fifteen years old, World War I broke out. The Netherlands stayed neutral; therefore Holland, as we also call our country, was never occupied. Despite the neutrality, the citizens of Holland were still affected. About a million Belgian citizens and soldiers fled to Holland, as did many soldiers from Germany. Because of the influx of fugitives, camps were set up throughout the country to feed and house them. One of these camps was in Groningen, not far from Oma's hometown, and also not far from the German border. Food was scarce because of the restrictions on trade with other countries. The country had to rely mainly on its own food resources. Oma lived in an agricultural area, where many fugitives were placed because food and shelter were available there.

Our little country of Holland went through many changes in its history. The Dutch are tough people who don't wear their hearts on their sleeves, but they willingly share whatever they have with others who are in need. That is still the case today.

Oma Tells Her Life Story

Once again I found myself by the fire at the cedar grove. As I arrived at the circle, I found the grandmothers waiting for me. After we settled in on our seats on the benches, the wise woman healer Tishie spoke. "Today it is Klazina's turn, the one you know as your oma, to tell her story. These flatlands in and around Sappemeer/Slochteren, where many of your ancestors were born," she continued, "were once a forest. Slochteren is a collection of villages now surrounded by agricultural flatlands. A part of the name indicates that a long time ago, this was a dense wooded area where pagans lived some forty-five hundred years ago. That's why we, your ancestors, decided to gather in these woods, since the ancient energy is still present. Here in the dream world, it is easier to connect with the ancient wise ones who still hold the sacred wisdom. Well-known in the history of our village was the worship of pagans celebrating Saint Magdalena, around the year 1500, in honor of the one you know from your Bible as the healer Mary Magdalene, who was a companion of Christ. This information shows the deep-rooted feminine dwellers in the area dating back to ancient times. That's why we are supportive of your journey. And we want to share our own account because we know we are all connected through what is recorded in the ancient text. We know that what happens to one woman is recorded in all of our memory cells from generation to generation. That is why it's important for us to support each other. Now let's continue sharing one of our sister's stories."

I noticed that Oma's appearance on the other side of the veil was once again very different from what it had been the other times we'd been together. I knew she'd noticed what I was thinking, because she said, "What you see in my appearance is a reflection of my life as Klazina. We can shape-shift into any figure we want to be at any time. In order for you to get the true feeling of my story, I decided to show you what my energy field looked like when I lived in the physical form.

"I married," she continued, "your grandfather Coenraad de Groot when I was eighteen years old. My first child, your aunt, was born in 1919. I was twenty years old by then. And two years later, the twins, your mom and her sister, were born. When the twins were almost six, their baby brother was born. He unfortunately died by drowning in a nearby ditch at age two in 1929. The grief I had to endure was unbearable. I remember vividly the moment I realized he was missing. Panic pierced my heart like a knife stabbing the life out of me. I knew in an instant what had happened. I knew he was gone. He had escaped me within seconds while I was peeling potatoes for our supper. He had fallen into the ditch close to our house. I don't remember where my thoughts had taken me, but in that split second, I knew something terrible had happened. I blamed myself for a long time. No matter what anyone said to me, there was no relief from the bondage I placed myself in. I slipped away in a dark alley of emotional depression, beating myself up for the loss of my precious child.

"Not long after, your grandfather and I were presented with the opportunity of a possible move to the western part of the country, far away from the horrible memories that kept me captive. Guilt-ridden, I felt I needed to stay, but I had no choice, because it was best for the family to move and easier to find work in the west. What troubled me most was the thought of leaving the place where my son died. I thought that once I left, I would abandon him again. Only parents who have lost a child can understand the hole the loss of a child leaves in their heart.

"Less than a year later, we moved to Den Helder, a city located on the west side of the country, because jobs were scarce in the area we lived in. At that time it was like emigrating from Europe to the United States, like you did in your lifetime. We didn't know if we would ever see again those whom we had left behind. To cope with the loss of my child and moving so far away from my family, I found peace in growing a garden. It was different from the countryside I had grown up in, where the land was plenty, but the new city provided community gardens so people could grow their own vegetables. Behind our house I found some room for a chicken coop. Growing a garden, raising chickens, and taking care of my girls helped me cope with the loss of my son. Knitting was one of my favorite hobbies that I joyfully practiced in the winter months, when the garden was at rest. I knitted sweaters, socks, baby clothes, and even skirts and dresses for my girls. But despite all of the distractions, there wasn't a day that went by when I wouldn't think about my son, especially on his birthday. Each year I would think about what he would look like and how his character would have developed.

"You could say I had my fair share of physical pain. I suffered from open sores on my legs, which led to my being hospitalized for six weeks at a time. They, the medical community, would clean and dress the wounds daily and cover me with a hoop so the sheets would not touch my legs. I had my legs always wrapped in gauze and had to wear heavy stockings. Since I didn't have diabetes, which was often a cause of my condition, the doctors suspected I had been exposed as a young child to chemicals used in the agricultural fields surrounding us, or poisoned plants or insects, but no doctor ever found out what it was that caused my sores. In my own limited mind, my physical pain told me I deserved to be punished for not saving my son. So I took the pain and carried it with me like a twisted badge of honor.

"When I was in my forties, the Second World War broke out. I often thought about my precious son and what it would have been like if he were still alive at that time. As a teenager he would have probably been taken away from us to work in the German camps like so many other young men had, many of them never returning to their parents. The fear my family and I went through during the war was tremendous. Two of my daughters lost their husbands. In the year 1943, my mother died at the age of seventy-nine. And my youngest brother, Paulinus Niewold, was killed by the Germans only months after Mother's passing. I almost lost a second child, your mom, to a bombing accident. Luckily I was spared this trauma. In the end, it was breast cancer that caused my death.

"I want to share one last thing about my passing," continued Oma. "When I died, I was greeted by the spirit of my son Eildert. He looked so vibrant and happy. He shared the following with me: 'Let me go back to the time I drowned,' he said. 'I watched you mourn my passing. What you didn't know was that my spirit was around you all the time, but you couldn't hear or feel me. I want you to know that I didn't suffer; on the contrary, my death was actually beautiful. I found myself surrounded by beautiful flowers; the colors were so vibrant that I can't even explain. The next thing I knew was that the colors of the flowers dissolved into beautiful spiritual beings of light, who greeted me with an indescribable love so great that I felt I had come home to the most glorious place. My drowning was just a freak accident. The ditch I stepped in to was covered with algae that looked to me like grass. I thought I could step on it, but as soon as I did, I fell into a dark hole, followed by seeing the flowers I described earlier. I want you to know that I would have died at an early age anyway, as I was only to be on earth for a short time. It is important for you to know that it was difficult to watch you feel so guilty, because it was not your fault. Other parents who have lost a child need to hear my story, because it is related to all of us kids who leave the earth early. There is always a reason for our leaving early that is part of our contract. Please tell parents not to feel guilty. You gave your children a beautiful experience of love, no matter how long we lived on the earthly plane. What is most important is that we feel that love from the moment we are born, and even before.'"

The next thing I knew, I was back in my body, feeling the sense of waking up from a dream.

Residue of a Lifetime

What Oma and I shared in our DNA was breast cancer. No matter what traumatic experiences we have endured, or the life-threatening diseases we deal with, there are always many levels of mental and emotional feelings we bear within the memory of our souls. In Oma's life's journey, the residue of how she perceived her physical diseases and the emotional trauma of losing her child and living through two wars has long been cleared away. That lifetime is now recorded in her Akashic archives as just a story, without the emotional charge. Although she is not affected anymore by the passage of that lifetime, the energy can still be picked up by those living on earth who share her genetic makeup. It is now up to us to consciously release these emotions of way back when that are imprinted on our physical DNA. We can learn to recognize what is ours and what is not. This takes practice, especially for the empathic, who is not always able to determine what is hers and what is not, but over time we can learn. At this moment in time, doors are opening for us to walk across the threshold and evolve. Part of evolving is being aware of our thoughts, emotions, and feelings. We are blessed with the omens, messages, and synchronicities our spiritual friends leave for us. It's up to us to open the doors and listen to the signs surrounding us. Only when we shine the light on past false impressions can we let go and free ourselves for the new mastery that is our birthright. That's how we are part of the new evolution that will shape humanity. When we change something within ourselves, it will ripple throughout the entire world.

Guided Imagery: Oma's Healing at the Circle

It was now my turn to bring Oma to the circle of healing. After I focused on my breathing and relaxed my entire body, I went into a trance and called upon her spirit to meet me in the woods by the fork in the road. When we met, I noticed that her appearance was different; she looked much like a wounded older woman. "I show you the condition my body was in before I died, holding all my sorrow in my memory cells. Let's walk on the path to the cedar grove, where the women are waiting for us." When we entered the sacred place, we were greeted by our ancestors with warm hearts. The wise woman Tishie, who was a healer in her lifetime, took Oma by the hand and led her to a place in the circle.

"We want you to watch closely and notice what's happening in your field while we work on her. The physical pain your oma endured," Tishie explained, "was a compilation of mental and emotional experiences in the life lived as Klazina. Because she perceived that no one cared about how she felt when she had pain, she developed a deep-rooted anger with a touch of unresolved fear that was never expressed. That anger contracted her muscles, leading to pain in the legs and open sores, creating a toxic reaction in her body. All her body was trying to do was to release the huge amount of trauma. Of course, at that time, no one had any idea about these body–mind connections. I could see a darkness surrounding her, representing her grief over the loss of her son lodged in her chest."

My oma said, "Sometimes when I thought about him, I felt a stabbing pain in my heart. In those moments I had difficulty breathing. All that fear, anger, and guilt was cleansed after I crossed over. By you being present and a witness to this process, you become a conduit. We clean your energy field, which still holds my life-experienced emotions as part of your genetic makeup. Remember that I, your oma, am free of the emotional traumas I lived through. For all of us at the circle, they are just stories of our history."

Tishie took Oma to a convertible table covered with blankets and pillows and asked her to lie down close to the fire. Then Tishie applied the oils of frankincense and eucalyptus to Oma's chest. Standing next to Tishie, I watched as the energy of the oils moved from Oma into my field. It was as if all the cells of my body received the vibration of the oils. I could smell the powerful fragrance. "These oils move through the blood–brain barrier, and from there into the bloodstream and all the memory cells of your DNA," said Tishie. "They have amazing healing properties, especially frankincense, which was given, as you might remember, to the baby Jesus at his birth. Eucalyptus opens the bronchial tubes and makes it easier to breathe." Next she placed the oil of rose on Oma's heart area. This oil has the highest frequency of love in the universe. All of a sudden the field around us changed into a fragrant garden of roses, releasing the energy of love and compassion. We watched Oma and the spirit of her son embrace each other, their fields bursting into a powerful rainbow of colors and light. "With this light we erase the emotions of grief and the thoughts and feelings of guilt from the entire genetic line," continued Tishie. Again I felt the cleansing in the core of my being. "Know that we are always together in spirit for eternity. Maybe we play different roles in the physical, but in spirit we are all one."

After the application of the oils, I could see a dark energy lifted from Oma's upper body. A ray of light was shining from above onto her chest. Next Tishie waved her hands down Oma's legs in a rotating motion. It was like rainbows of lights appeared from the center of her hands. She moved her hands until the dark spots disappeared. I could feel the waving energy move through my own legs. Tishie showed how to look for the colors and asked the women to create a field of compassion to visualize healing energy emerging from the light.

"This is what happens when healers use energy work," she said, "except that in the physical world, most people are not able to see the colors or light." Finally the women gathered in a circle around Oma and me, and then Tishie taught us fitting affirmations in a song related to the healing at hand. In unity we sang a mantra: "All gone, all cleared, for all generations to be free."

An Imprint of Guilt, Breast Cancer

Breast cancer was imprinted in my memory cells long before it manifested in my body. When Oma had breast cancer, her journey was not an easy one. I remember visiting her in the medical ward of the senior citizens' facility where she lived. One night in 1973, a few weeks before her passing, she was in a great deal of pain lying in her hospital bed. She asked me to find a nurse, saying that she was hurting so bad that she couldn't stand it anymore. None of the nurses had responded to her call for help. I noticed her left arm was very swollen and red, and I could see the pain written on her face. I went out to find a nurse, but all the halls of the medical facility were empty. There was no nurse to be found. With a heavy heart, I returned to Oma's room, feeling guilty and ashamed that I couldn't help her. Minutes later, what seemed like hours, a nurse came in and gave Oma medicine to ease her pain. Soon Oma relaxed and fell asleep. With a heavy heart filled with guilt, I left her that night. It was the last time I would see her alive. Ever since that day, I have carried the guilt I felt at that moment in time. It lodged itself like a heavy rock in my stomach. I had subconsciously buried that pain for all these years, up until now.

Guided Imagery: Releasing Guilt

One night just before I fell asleep, Oma's spirit dropped in. "Guess what we need to talk about?" said the voice of Oma. "It's time to visit the past and to remember what happened so we can release it. I followed her in anticipation and was somewhat alarmed by her approach, realizing the heaviness of that guilt she held. "First of all," she continued, "that pain you witnessed was mine to carry, not yours. Second, because of that specific experience of seeing me suffer, your subconscious mind decided that one day you would choose to help people by making them feel better." Holy moly, that really hit home. This was one of those moments when all of a sudden a light goes on, a big light. I could feel her smile upon me, and I knew at that particular moment that something profound had happened.

Next, in my mind's eye I saw us walking in the magical woods. Oma was wearing a dark blue robe, and around her waist was hanging a small burlap bag, one she would gather herbs in. She leaned on a walking stick decorated with carvings, rocks, feathers, ribbons, and crystals—a much different sight from how the garment I remembered her wearing during our first visit. Then she gestured for me to follow her. We entered the familiar cedar grove in the clearing of the woods. I loved the smell of the sacred trees. Our place of gathering became my second home, my home away from home. The fire was burning and the grandmothers were gathered around. I was welcomed with joy by every woman's spirit, including my mother's, who said, "Come, stand here by the fire and feel the love of your grandmothers holding you in this sacred place." I had never experienced to be unconditional loved by so many powerful spiritual beings at one time. The women began to chant. Some were holding crystals; others, incense. Oma held a beautiful feather in her hand and waved it back and forth over me.

"Today we release from your cells the emotions from the memory of guilt. Cleansing these emotions will not only free your field but also make room for the next generations to start with a clean slate free of guilt." A heavy weight was lifted from my stomach area. All the women gathered around me, holding me in the sacred light of spirit. I felt much different than I had felt before entering the circle. I felt whole, like the light of God was shining directly upon me. After the ceremony, each of the women blessed me with their presence, love, and wisdom. Then we celebrated with dance and song.

Mom and Oma were the first two of my seven ancestors who shared their stories with me at the circle. Of the seven generations, they are the only ones whom I had known in my lifetime. I felt blessed to have been their daughter and granddaughter and the recipient of the wisdom they shared with me. If it hadn't been for my cancer diagnosis, I probably would never have connected with my grandmother's spirit this way. Both my sister and I were gifted with spiritual guidance throughout our cancer journeys that gave us a renewed closeness between each other and a new perspective on life, one we never would have had otherwise.

The most revelatory fact I learned at the circle was that when we pass over to the other side of the veil, we cleanse the emotions connected to the lifetime just lived, and all there is left is that life's story, which is then deposited in the Akashic records. This especially made sense to me when I realized that each soul has many lifetimes recorded in its Akash. It would be overwhelming to feel all the emotions of each lifetime, which could be in the thousands. I wondered where these emotions resided and learned that they are stored in us, their descendants, in the cells of our DNA. Not only are they stored there, but also they are recorded in the grid lines covering the earth, in the places where people leave the imprints of their experiences. That's why people can feel energy and emotions sometimes when they go to places where remnants of a disaster can still be detected by a sensitive person. What is interesting is that when we release these emotions from our cells, we not only clear our own genetic makeup and that of our family members but also free the grid of the earth from energies stored in places where disasters took place. This is how the vibration of earth and humankind is transforming into a new positive energy.

The residue of my ancestors' stories is still in the energy field of my genetic makeup, as well as in the genes of my children, grandchildren, siblings, and cousins. That's why it's so important to free ourselves from these old energies, because we have never been at this point in human history before, where so much new data is available to us. Our brains are overloaded with new information, and therefore we cannot afford to hold on to our outdated ancestral experiences. I feel I have already cleared a great deal since I have been writing about my family, but I know I still have a long way to go to be healed. It's a start; I have to begin somewhere. This is how I choose to embark on my new journey. I hope something new is birthed for me and for all my relations.

For you, my dear reader, I hope you will find healing in the next part of *Visitors along My Cancer Journey*, where the next five generations of my ancestors not only share their stories of distress but also take you to the circle to heal and to release the old energies from your genetic cells, where they don't belong. Let my ancestors' words ring through when they say, "We no longer have any emotion to deal with on this side of the veil. Our question is, why should you?"

Part II

Part II

Chapter 6

Trauma Caused by Rape

Ariella Atwood, Born in 1749 in Dorking, England

Generational Imprints

The cedar grove became a sacred sanctuary for me to go. Not only did I meet my ancestors at this magical place, but also I learned from them how my personal conflicts are often directly linked to their stories. It was now time to hear the stories of the next five generations in line. From deep inside of me, spiritual and pagan traditions of healing emerged, leading me to study alternative medicine. *Could it be,* I wondered, *that I have been guided all along by my ancestors and have just now discovered this?* I now realize that many of my interests in life stem from generational imprints left in my DNA. That being the case, I want to know how to tune in to what is recorded in my field and learn how to either release that which is not working for me or enhance what is. Here is where the connection of my grandmothers is very powerful, as not only had I learned about their stories still present in my genes, but also they guide me to release the residue left in my cells.

Through research and from meditation, I discovered an old connection to a faraway relation, a woman pilgrim named Priscilla Mullins who came to North America on the *Mayflower*. I noticed many synchronicities with her. We were both immigrants departing from Holland to the United States, and like her I consider myself a member of a new spiritual movement very much in tune with God but not directed by the dogma of any church. Priscilla was born in Surrey,

England, in a town named Dorking. Her father, William Mullins, was a shopkeeper, but he left England with his wife, Alice Atwood, and their two youngest children, who hadn't reached adulthood yet, because of a disagreement with the principles of the Church of England. William and Alice became members of the new English separatist church and felt persecuted by the leaders of the old church. They fled to Holland, a country more tolerant and accepting of different ways of thinking, something that is still true today. From there they boarded the ship the *Mayflower*, taking them to their new country. Pilgrims, as they were later called, started their new church in their new country, with freedom to practice their faith. They followed the old rituals of the seasons by planting and harvesting crops in relation to the positions of the stars. Like the pagans they celebrated seasonal ceremonial festivals and other old folkloric festivals dating back to ancient times, before churches were established. Looking back at Priscilla's life, I feel that we have come full circle, weaving all of our stories into a tapestry of the history of the genetic line we are part of. Within these universal threads we share a new spiritual evolution. What we have in general is a new way of living according to our own spirituality like the first pilgrims did, instead of following the outdated rules of religion. Having said that, I think churches are still very important, because they are a place where people still find God. The energy of spirit is still present in church buildings. On top of this, it doesn't matter where people find God. That spiritual energy is universal, something we all share in the genes of our family histories. The human experience of today is guiding us into the new evolution of humankind by teaching us to accept our differences and to have compassion for our fellow citizens even if they show their darkness to us, keeping in mind that at the end, in the presence of our light, darkness cannot exist.

The cedar grove was calling me. I settled in, starting to relax myself through breathing, and sitting in front of my altar with sacred objects like candles, incense, and crystals. Soon I relaxed in deep meditation, finding my way to my grandmothers, who were waiting by the fire. The aroma of incense filled the air. Before I entered the circle, I was smudged with sage to clear my field.

Now is the time when we will listen to the stories of my next five ancestors, starting with the one farthest back in history.

Ella's Story: The Early Years

Ella introduced herself, showing her essence as a young blonde maiden with blue eyes. "Long ago," she stated, "my story emerged on the outskirts of Dorking, a small village in Surrey, England, south of London. I remember sitting on the tiny front porch of our humble cottage stringing beans for our family supper meal. Over the summer months, my sister Lizzy and I harvested most of the vegetables from the family garden, except for the winter crops such as brussels sprouts, kale, and cabbage, which were still in the garden. These vegetables were to be harvested later because they tasted much better after the first overnight frost had covered them with a white dusting of ice. Lizzy and I had already packed three gallon jars of pickles, while our older sisters Willow and Brandy had carefully hung the onions and garlic up to dry.

"I can easily imagine the delicious aromas of my favorite fall and winter meal: meat stew loaded with carrots, potatoes, turnips, and onions. Those smells would always permeate the whole house. Coal was expensive and had to be used sparingly, so after an hour of cooking the stew, Mother would wrap the hot pot in cloths and then carefully place the whole thing in one of the beds and cover it with woolen blankets, keeping the stew at a slow brew all day long until suppertime. My empty stomach rumbled, bringing me back to the task at hand."

A New Opportunity

'Ella!' my mother called from the kitchen as the last bean dropped into the bucket. Wondering what my next chore might be, I grabbed the finished project and hurried in. It was a surprise to see my father sitting at the kitchen table.

'Mother and I want to speak with you,' Dad announced. 'You're thirteen years old. Mother doesn't need your help as much this fall. William is now eighteen months, and Miles is already three years old. I've found a marvelous situation for you as chambermaid for the Cook household.; He paused and looked straight at me. 'You pay attention and make yourself useful. I've given my word. Make this family proud. Mr. Cook is president of one of the most important businesses in town. He must be the wealthiest of citizens, and holds a strong influence in our community.'

"Relentless in his gaze, my father waited for my response. 'Oh! I will! I will!' I proclaimed with all the determination I could muster, as if my life depended on it.

"When I left the kitchen, a huge smile spread across my face. I could not believe my good fortune. It was a dream come true. I would be on my own for the first time, and away from the only life I had ever known. It was a wonderful opportunity to find my identity, independence, and self-worth. No one understood my true feelings, thoughts, and dreams of being connected with spirit. Now I would have an opportunity to discover a new outlook on the way other people lived. I dreamed about seeing the big house full of colors, fine linen, china, and beautiful gowns with jewels collected from exciting places beyond the sea. There had to be more to life than living in a puny cottage. I wanted to break the chains of poverty that had been present for generations in my family, not only for me but also for all of my siblings.

"The following day I was up before the sun to get ready for my walk to my new job. There was no mistaking the Cooks' stately manor located in the best part of town, only a short distance from Dorking's center. It was a brisk walk in the chilly morning air, but I did not notice because I was both nervous and excited, my mind wandering to what lay ahead. It wasn't long until I approached the front of the mansion. I decided to stop for a peek through the rod-iron gate. I was impressed by such a grand palace. Not being allowed to use the front entrance, I walked around to a narrow path leading to the back alley.

"It was not yet seven in the morning as I stood at the rear entrance, which was the only door servants were allowed to use. My knees shaking, and with a trembling hand, I rang the doorbell and waited. There was only silence. Suddenly the door flew open. Before me stood a tall, sturdy but slim, gray-haired lady whom I surmised was probably in her fifties. She wore an immaculate uniform. Her facial expression remained frozen as if she had forgotten how to smile. She glared up and down at me with cold, stony gray eyes, assessing her new trainee.

Speaking in a low-pitched articulate voice and with a stern tone, she said, 'I'm Miss Wellbee. I've been the main housekeeper for the Cooks for many years. You'll obey my orders. If you do as I say, you'll do fine. *If not*, you'll be out of here in a week.' She started to turn, but then she stopped and looked me straight in the eyes, declaring in a firm, commanding tone, 'The most important rule of the household is that the chamber help is never allowed to be in the living quarters when the family is home. Don't you ever forget!'

"It wasn't so much the words but the demeaning tone and superior attitude that startled me. Miss Wellbee definitely gave the impression that she was of a higher class than I, a simple soul from the outskirts of town. An alarm went off inside. A strong sinking feeling made me wonder about this place of sparkle and glitter. Perhaps it might be different than I had imagined.

"Hurrying to catch up with Miss Wellbee, who was already halfway down the hall, I noticed that the head housekeeper was limping. The same expression of pain that had overwhelmed my father at times was evident in her gait. In the dimly lit hallway, I could see her energy field blotched with darkness. It was as if Miss Wellbee was protecting herself from something. Maybe she was not as tough as she appeared? *Her position of responsibility must weigh heavy upon her shoulders,* I concluded. Remembering what my mother had taught me about compassion, I vowed to work hard and earn the head housekeeper's respect. Perhaps then I could relate on more friendly terms.

"Entering the large kitchen, I was impressed with huge pots and pans hanging from the ceiling, sizable work counters, and a gigantic hearth on one side. The welcoming aroma of freshly baked breads made my stomach rumble. There I met the other employees. As I sipped some tea and gobbled up a freshly baked biscuit with jam, I felt a little better knowing I did not have to face Miss Wellbee all by myself. I tried to bury my uneasy concerns, rationalizing that I was merely nervous and overreacting.

'Follow me.' The head housekeeper led me down to the basement stairs to a small cubicle with a dresser and a cot, with one small window allowing some warmth from its southern exposure. 'This is your room. Change and return promptly,' she ordered, handing me a crisp new uniform. I dressed quickly and instantly loved my simple but neat black uniform with its heavily starched white apron.

'Come with me upstairs to the library. I want to introduce you to Mr. Cook. Mind you, be sure to curtsy and bow. Do not speak. A maid must be seen but not heard,' instructed Miss Wellbee as we walked up the broad curved stairway.

"The head housekeeper suddenly halted before entering the library. She stood a little taller and squared her shoulders as if bracing to confront an enemy. *Strange behavior*, I thought. Proceeding inside, we stopped a ways back from a huge cherrywood desk. 'Mr. Cook, beg pardon for the interruption.; Her voice strained, Miss Wellbee continued. 'Presenting Miss Atwood, the new chambermaid. I shall see that she is properly trained for her station.' As she waved her hand toward her new hire, I curtsied and bowed.

"Miss Wellbee backed up a couple of feet as Mr. Cook scooted back his chair, stood up, and came around in front of the desk. He was short, balding, and stout. His eyes were half hidden behind round spectacles. Despite the pink blush of his face, his expression seemed dark and foreboding. I became alarmed as I caught a glimpse of his colors. They were murky greens, reds, and brown in dark tones such as I had not seen before. Mr. Cook slowly circled around me. I could smell an awful mixture of cigar and alcohol. I sensed his eyes scanning me up and down. I felt uncomfortable and degraded but could not understand why. He stopped and looked me in the eye, a look I had never known before but definitely did not like. 'She'll do,' he stated. Miss Wellbee nudged my arm, and we withdrew from the room.

"As the weeks passed, I became used to the routine of the household chores. I concentrated carefully on every instruction and detail. I worked hard cleaning, cooking, and performing many other duties. All things considered, I was pleased with my grand place of employment and its extra benefits, which included my small room with a cot in the basement and three very good meals daily. Sometimes the Cooks would even send delicacies home with me when I would go home for my weekly visits to the family. I refused to allow my thoughts to review that appalling experience in the library. Yet I made very sure to stay clear of the master of the house.

"February was ending. The first signs of spring were in the air. I always loved the early birds' singing at morning's first awakening in the garden. I could see crocus and daffodils stretching their leaves through the retreating snow. On this sunny afternoon, I felt lucky to work outside cleaning the front cobblestones. My mind traveled back over the last few months. This winter I had experienced the beginning of my menses. At first I was frightened, but then I remembered a secret conversation with my sister Lizzy. I realized I was becoming a woman. An awareness of pride and accomplishment had welled up inside, which showed in my attitude and in my work. I began to feel secure in my position and experienced a sense of belonging to the group of people with whom I labored. It had taken five months of working, but I finally seemed to have earned the approval of Miss Wellbee. I figured that perhaps the old maid had never married because she always appeared to be so angry and distrustful of people."

The Trauma Caused by Rape

"One day, Miss Wellbee ordered me to place new bedsheets in the sleeping quarters of Mr. and Mrs. Cook. It was already late morning. Lady Cook had taken her time getting dressed and had left just a few minutes prior. She was probably headed for a luncheon meeting with her friends and wouldn't be back until she was done with high tea at the club. I needed to have everything completed before Mr. Cook arrived home at noon for lunch, because afterward he always took a nap prior to returning to his work. I had always made sure never to be in the living quarters when the family was home. It was the essential rule. I immediately grabbed my dusting cloth, broom, and sheets, and rushed upstairs to finish my duties.

"I gathered up the missus' dirty clothes, quickly swept the floor, and dusted. Of course, in my haste, I was careless with the tucking in of the front corner of the bottom sheet, so it was not folded securely. When I pulled to tighten the sheet, it flew off the bed, throwing me onto the floor. Frustrated, I struggled to my feet. I started making the bed over again, just as the grandfather clock in the library began to chime, eventually sounding twelve times. I scrambled to finish, grabbed the dirty laundry, and turned to review my work, when I was startled by the sound of footsteps coming up the stairs. I became alarmed. I had to get out—now!

"Blocking my exit, Mr. Cook stood squarely in the doorway. A dark cloud engulfed his colors. Flashing flecks of red shot out of his eyes like lightning bolts. A wicked smile curled across his flushed face, and a dirty chuckle rose from deep in this throat as he recognized in me his young prey. His eyes glared at me and seemed to be on fire. I struggled to avoid his piercing gaze, stammered an apology, and attempted to get by him and through the doorway.

"The master of the house closed the door and slid the lock in place behind him. A feeling of panic overwhelmed me as he grabbed my arms and threw me on the bed. With his hand over my mouth, he ordered me to be quiet and not to say anything. I froze. I was terrified and felt defenseless. I closed my eyes, wishing I would wake up from a terrible dream, but the horror continued. His body weighed heavily upon mine. I had to force myself to inhale. But when I did, the smells were awful. His clothing reeked of atrocious cigar fumes. His hot breath in my face was heavy with the stench of alcohol, and then from somewhere came a disgusting stinky sweaty scent. I felt lightheaded and wished I could escape, but to no avail. Everything went so fast that I didn't understand what had happened. All I could feel was a sharp pain between my legs.

"After the lord of the manor was done, he ordered me to change the sheets because of the bloody stains. He pulled up his britches, preparing to leave, when he abruptly halted. In a hoarse whisper, Mr. Cook declared, 'Don't say a bloody word about what just happened, or else you'll lose your job. Your father'll be out of work as well. Your family'll be in distressing circumstances, and it'll all be *your* fault!'

"The door slammed shut. I found myself shaking, with tears welling up in my eyes. I hurriedly adjusted my uniform and set about changing the sheets once again. I somehow forced myself to complete the rest of the assigned duties for the day as though nothing had happened.

"For days I felt that I was living in a fog. I had no idea what made my insides hurt so terribly. I was conscious of a dirty, unclean feeling that could not be washed away with soap and water. I followed my daily routine, but the luster and allure of the grand illusion of wealth had been shattered. The fine furniture, delicate china, and shiny silver no longer enticed my daydreams. How had my happiness been ripped from me? I did not know; I only knew that it was gone. I felt all alone in the world. There was no one with whom to share this dreadful experience. I feared losing my job and causing my father to be dismissed, which would leave my family destitute. It was *my* entire fault. So I buried the unspeakable experience deep inside. No one would ever know of the dreadful deed that I had done ...

"Months passed, spring had vanished, and summer flowers were already in full bloom. I had not taken any notice. I tried hard to avoid Mr. Cook as much as I could. Even a glimpse of him reminded me of that horrible day upstairs in the bedroom. Yet there were those unavoidable moments when his victorious glare made something inside me die a little more. I kept my distance from my fellow workers, minimizing conversation, and looked away whenever Miss Wellbee sent an inquiring gaze. I had become depressed and quiet, focusing solely on my assigned tasks. Most of the time I did a great job of ignoring the nagging emotions that plagued me. Life went on all around me, but my joyful character was deeply damaged.

"Then one day I noticed on one of my visits home that my mother's demeanor toward me had changed. Could she have found out what had happened? I felt so guilty. I could not bear the thought that my mother, whom I loved and respected very much, would turn against me in shame. I tried hard to find another reason why she had been looking so sad lately. Mother appeared distracted and deep in thought. Something was definitely bothering her. What if she was sick? As a child, I'd often had strong feelings about things that would happen. What I felt now was fear, but I had no reason as to why. The only thing I knew was that something serious was going on at home.

"On my weekly visits to the family, Mother often asked me if I was all right. I tried to sound cheerful to reassure my mother that I was fine. I went through a rough spot in the spring. For a couple of months I thought I had a persisting stomach flu, but it disappeared by itself. I had felt a little queasy, but that was probably because of the hard work. I had also noticed the increase of a few pounds, which, I reasoned, looked good on me since I had always been on the skinny side. The abundant food at the Cooks' house made me look healthier."

The Revelation

"A couple of weekends later, on my next visit home, after a very quiet dinner, I was directed by my parents into their bedroom. As I walked in, I felt a rush of heavy energy encapsulating my entire body. My father closed the door behind me and gestured for me to sit down on the side of the bed. It felt like I was in deep trouble, yet I had no idea what I possibly could have done wrong. They had no way of knowing what had happened to me some six months ago. Father looked angry, and my mother was sad. Mother looked down to the floor to avoid facing me. She sat in the corner chair. Father took charge and started to speak in a deep authoritative voice with a dead-serious tone. He demanded me to reveal my secret boyfriend. He needed to know his name so he could discuss with him this critical subject. I didn't understand the question my father asked or the tone in which he spoke. What was this critical subject about? I did not have time for boyfriends and simply was not interested in boys.

'Father,' I said, 'I really don't have a boyfriend, and I don't know what serious matter you want to talk about.' I had never been in trouble. I pondered what it could possibly be that was so horrible. Could they have heard the horrible thing that happened to me at the Cooks' house?

"Furious at such indiscretion, my frustrated father raised his voice. 'Your mother thinks you are with child, and you need to have been with a man to become pregnant.' It seemed to me that my father's light colors were being consumed by huge red flames. I had no idea why he would be so angry. I had no boyfriend and did not know what 'being with child' meant. How could anything have happened?

'You have to believe me,' I cried out. 'I have no boyfriend.'

"My father grabbed me by the arms and called me a liar. 'I am not lying! I speak the truth!' I declared.

"Then all of a sudden I had a flashback that triggered a vision of that horrible day when Mr. Cook hurt me, grabbing me by the arms like my father had done just now. I gasped and stammered, 'Mr. Cook did something to me that was painful and made me bleed.'

'You are lying! I want you out of here! Be gone by tomorrow! I never want to see your face again in this household! From now on you are on your own!' he exclaimed. Then he stomped out, slamming the door behind him.

'Please! Papa, please!' I begged, attempting to control my sobbing. 'I had to promise Mr. Cook not to speak to anyone about the matter or else I'd lose my position, and you'd be out of work as well, which would make the entire family suffer and it'd be my entire fault!'

"Devastated, I fell to the floor. I felt my mother's arms surrounding me. Both of us were weeping now. No words were spoken. The house grew quiet. For moments it felt as though we were all alone in a world of deep darkness. For some time, Mom held me in her arms, rocking me back and forth like she had done when I was little. 'It's okay, my baby,' she repeatedly said. 'I believe you.' We both cried for the injustice done to me."

Lost and Alone

"Early in the morning following my father's declaration, before darkness would be replaced by dawn, and long before the family would awaken, I departed alone. I was filled with shame and confusion, questioning my fate. There was not even an opportunity to say goodbye to my siblings. My mother was the only one bidding me farewell. She gave me directions to follow the road in the woods leading to the cabin where I would find a woman healer who lived there. I was to stay with her and have my child. My mother held me for what felt like an hour, then she handed me a small bundle with a loaf of bread, a couple of slices of cheese, and a handful of freshly picked fruits for my journey into the forest.

"Scared and alone, I followed the path that had been trodden down by use. As my journey progressed, until the first light of dawn, which revealed the direction ahead, I pondered my terrible turn of fortune. I felt lost, having been forced to leave the security of my family and my home without a proper situation in life or an identity of my own. I did not really understand what had gone wrong. Even worse, I had no inkling of what to do beyond this point. Before the confrontation with my father, I had thought my life to be pleasant and agreeable, offering opportunities of accomplishment, but now I realized that I had greatly shamed my family. How could I bring this child into a world of disgrace? How could I possibly care for the infant? It was all very overwhelming to consider and too much for me to handle. The only life I knew was gone. All I wanted was to die and be at peace. Yet for some reason I continued on the path before me.

"At midafternoon, the trail widened and the rays of the sun revealed a clearing ahead, with a small cabin at its center. As I drew closer, I could see a rainbow of flowers bordering a garden on the south. The tiny yard was neat and carefully woven among the established trees, appearing not to disturb the natural order of things, which under different circumstances would have pleased me. However, without regard to my surroundings, I focused solely on the unknown before me. My knees were shaking as I forced myself to knock on the front door. My future had been cast into the hands of someone I did not know, a fate of destiny over which I had no control.

"Then a voice from behind surprised me. 'I have been expecting you.' A woman with long dark hair and dark brown eyes came up the walkway. She was dressed in a colorful skirt with many pockets and an oversized shirt that was not flattering. It was a far cry from the style of Mrs. Cook and her friends, but this woman's demeanor was friendly and personable. With her arms filled with firewood, she nodded for me to open the door. 'I'm Lorrie,' she said invitingly. 'C'mon in and make y'rself at home. Place your belongings in the corner while I kindle the fire.'

"While I was waiting for another order, Lorrie turned around and, with love in her eyes, welcomed me into her home. She placed her hands on my pregnant belly and continued. 'You'll have a little baby girl. We are going to welcome her into this world with love.'

"These words were the first kind words I had heard in a while. I fell into the arms of the older woman, crying and thinking of the injustice done to me, and the pain and shame I had brought upon my family. I didn't know what to think. The only thing I knew was that God and everyone else had left me alone with my misery. Stripped of my identity and the chance of a fulfilling life, I knew that I would never be able to face my family again. Nor would I ever again set foot in my beloved town.

"I slowly got used to my new surroundings. A couple of months after arriving at Lorrie's, I gave birth to a healthy baby girl, whom I named Maike. At first I did not want anything to do with my child, but the strict yet loving voice of Lorrie persuaded me to stay focused and care for the child. Still, life was never the same after the horrible experiences I had endured.

Taking My Own Life

"Life went on. Nevertheless, I never seemed to get back that spark of free spirit I'd had as a child. The only thing that nurtured me was walking in the woods by myself, with my bare feet on Mother Earth. Lorrie was the only mother figure I had now, but in the end, Lorrie's loving energy and that of my baby girl was not enough to keep me on this earthly plane. I slowly wasted away with an unbearable sadness. I was stripped of my youth; I missed my momma and sisters terribly; and I thought I was unable to blossom into womanhood. Then one day when I was in a deeply depressed place, a voice guided me to go to the woods. While there, I wept uncontrollably and fell onto Mother Earth, shaking, losing control of my thinking, falling into an even darker place. Next thing I noticed, there were poisonous plants growing right beside me, inviting me to pick them and eat them. After I did so, violent pains in my abdomen ripped my insides apart. In a strange way I welcomed this suffering, feeling it was the only way to escape my misery. Soon I lost consciousness. The next thing I knew, I was escorted into the light."

A View from Heaven

"After I arrived in heaven, I looked back at my life and watched the darkness that had surrounded me on earth being lifted off me. The next thing I knew, I was welcomed by my spirit ancestors and many beings of light. My mind was clear. I felt I had arrived home where I belonged. The pain was gone, the emptiness having been filled with love. Over time the broken pieces were put back together to make me whole again.

"From this new place I watched how my experience affected others. I realized that this trauma had not only happened to me; it had also happened to my parents. Now I watched from above how my death broke their hearts and how they lived with guilt and fear in their hearts for the rest of their lives.

"Besides my parents' pain, my passing also affected Lorrie, who was devastated by my death. *How could I have missed the signs of despair the young girl suffered?* she thought. Earlier she had had a vision of my passing, but she was too involved with the new baby, who already showed signs of the gift of a light being. I had lost the will to live and had no family unit where I was part of. The events I had endured left me without roots; I did not belong anywhere, not even in the woods with my baby girl! Lorrie sent a messenger to my parents with the sad news. Mom and Dad arrived the next day full of grief.

"When they received the bad news of my passing, I watched my dad's thoughts going back to that dreadful night when he sent me away. Deep down inside, he knew that I had spoken the truth about the rape by Mr. Cook, but he told himself that there was nothing else he could have done. His choice had been to send me away and save his livelihood and that of his family. He knew that Mr. Cook had a lot of power in the community. If my father would have confronted him with this issue, Mr. Cook would have made it very difficult for him to earn enough income to support his family and survive through the times in which they lived."

"Then I watched Mother, who could not stop sobbing. She felt very guilty about the way the family had treated me and about having rejected her own daughter. It seemed unfair that women could be abused and nobody in the world would give a hoot. She thought that men in power could get away with anything, even murder, which she felt had been done to her daughter.

"On the day my parents arrived in the cabin in the woods, they met their granddaughter for the first time. She looked exactly like me with big blue eyes and curly blonde hair. They looked upon my body, which lay on a beautiful altar filled with flowers. The maidens of Lorrie's community had placed flowers and ribbons in my hair and dressed me in a white satin gown. Beauty was all around. My parents were supported in a loving, respectful way by people whom they had never met but who celebrated my life in their special pagan way. The ceremony that followed was very graceful; they sang lovely songs with lyrics that sounded like an ancient language.

"After the ceremony, Bert and Mary talked to Lorrie about the future of their granddaughter. They said that they would not have any way to take care of this little one who looked so much like their daughter, and that she was a painful reminder of the suffering their daughter had endured. So it was decided that the young child, Maike, would be raised by Lorrie as her own."

Lessons from Beyond

"From my new home I watched the ceremony of my burial on the other side of the veil. The painful grief I watched my parents move through was difficult to witness. Tears welled in my eyes. In that moment, everything was made clear to me as I watched my energy field. I learned I was to observe my child's journey until she was grown before I could move on to my next spiritual lesson. All victims of suicide move through the same holding pattern, watching their loved ones and witnessing how life down on earth evolves without them. This is part of the contract we have with our loved ones. We are still connected with them for the rest of their lives on earth.

"By gaining a better understanding of what my actions had caused for others, my spirit council showed me how the choices I had mad impacted the lives of my parents. They showed me how Dad had processed the awful moment when he learned what had happened to me. He realized how dreadful it must have been for me, and he recognized that his frustration over the whole situation, and his actions toward me at that moment, had been directed only by his fear. He instantly knew there was no way to accuse my abuser. If he were to do so, his entire family would be destroyed, because no one could fight against a powerful man like Mr. Cook. I also watched the moment when I begged my father to believe me and saw how he cringed when standing behind the door after I'd called him Papa. Yet there was nothing he could have done to right this wrong perpetrated upon me. His fearful mind told him that yes, Mr. Cook would crush him and, of course, deny any wrongdoing toward his daughter. I, Ella, would be blemished forever. It would be best for all, he thought, if I left to have

73

my baby elsewhere. The thought of humiliation falling upon him and his family made him shudder through the core of his being.

"I was shown Mother's experience with Mr. Cook as a young woman. She remembered meeting him for the first time. He'd eyed her body up and down. She felt he was a creepy man, but she never expected he would one day abuse one of her daughters. For her it was difficult to process this trauma. She'd had no idea how to help me. Dad had asked her to make arrangements for me to go away, so she had walked to the woman in the woods who was called the witch doctor. Lorrie the healer agreed to take me in so that the baby could arrive safely in her sanctuary in the woods.

"Then I witnessed Mom falling apart while telling the story of my abuse to Lorrie. The healer felt very angry about the way some prominent men in their community misused power. 'If people could only understand the sacredness of mating energy, they would not have the desire to use an innocent girl barely capable of producing a child in her underdeveloped body,' she said. In her secret society of priestesses, they practiced sacred communion with their fellow priests to bring forth a blending of male and female energy, which join together as one to serve the Goddess. This energy was used to bring forth unconditional love and extend out into the natural world, to bring balance and peace through all. These practices were hundreds of years old, originating with early pagan society.

"Lorrie remembered that a long time ago, a young woman had come to her for the same type of trouble I had experienced with the same man. Her name was Ruby Wellbee. Ruby was very angry with her abuser and decided to punish him. She threatened him, demanding that he give her a secure job or else would tell the businessman's wife what had happened. Unfortunately, she had no idea that she had set herself up for a lifetime of anger and control that crippled her physically, mentally, and emotionally. Lorrie felt bad for Mary, who was devastated by the injustice done to her daughter and also understood the father's dilemma of possibly losing his livelihood if he were to confront a powerful man like Mr. Cook. Lorrie knew the predicament my parents faced and that they were devastated.

"After viewing my life, I started slowly drifting back to my new surroundings, this beautiful, peaceful place. I learned how my actions had caused others a great deal of pain, and now I had the responsibility of watching how their lives evolved without me. If I could reverse the decision I'd made on that dreadful day, I would do so, but it was too late for me. Hopefully it will not be for others. I decided at that moment that I would dedicate myself in spirit to those on earth who suffer like I did and hopefully make a difference in someone else life."

Guided Imagery: Releasing Trauma

When Ella finished her story, I could still smell the aroma of incense and sage hanging in the air around us. I vividly remembered my visit to the other side of the veil and noticed that the darkness of Ella's story of suicide and sexual abuse was still present in my genetic makeup.

The grandmothers helped me relax into a deeper state of consciousness and guided me to enter a sacred temple that had the form of a pyramid. When I made my entrance, I noticed a crystal table in the center of the space. Imprinted on the table were sacred geometric symbols designed just for me. The grandmothers gestured for me to lie down on the table. To my surprise, the crystal was pleasant, cool, and soft. Now the blueprint of my body with all its meridians, chakras, and genetic lines was aligned with the geometric symbols on the table. Above me I could see the sky, as the cap of the pyramid was removed and rainbow-colored rays of light shone down upon me, connecting me with all the sacred geometric symbols from above to below. I was surrounded by beings of light who guided me in meditation. A voice said that the negative memories of abuse and suicide were deleted from my body's cells, and not only from my personal blueprint but also from the memory cells of all women living on earth who had suffered the same as Ella. I felt a shiver in the fibers of my being, letting me know that this release was real. And so the stories of abuse lost their power, and the emotions were gone and deleted from the core of my being.

Somehow I was transported back to the circle, where the grandmothers created a sacred place for all women who have had the experience of abuse to be liberated from their painful memories forever. We prayed for all who suffered from mental instability and who had thoughts of committing suicide. Next we imagined that the energy cleared at the circle was received by the spirits of the flames of the fire. These spirits took the transformed images into the vortex. Then the images trickled down onto the earth, and from there into the grid lines that covered the planet. Then the message dispersed all over the world, connecting and supporting with those in need of letting go of their trauma. Last we visualized that unconditional love would find all who had suffered a similar trauma and transform these dear souls into the powerful human beings they were born to be.

Chapter 7

Choice between Good and Bad

Maike Atwood, Born in 1763 Near London, England

Once again I was ready to receive information from one of my ancestors. This time it was Maike, the daughter of Ella, whose story would be told at the circle.

Maike's Story: A Troubled Past

Maike, pronounced "M-eye-Kah," showed herself as a young woman with curly blonde hair and oval-shaped blue eyes. She was dressed in a dark purple velvet dress, finished with black lace at the end of her sleeves and the bottom of her skirt. Over her dress she wore a dark purple cape matching the fabric of her outfit. To finish the look, she showed off her black laced boots in accordance with the style of that time. She looked stunning in a dark kind of way, wicked and kind of mysterious to say the least. "I show you how this dark purple outfit matched my character, especially in my younger years, so you get the sense of the way I lived and behaved as an angry child and later an angry woman trained in the mystical traditions who struggled with the duality of genetic traits I inherited from both my parents. I discovered at a young age the story of how I was conceived, and from there I made up my young naive mind that my father was a terrible person and my mother was a saint. While I had never met either my mom or my dad, I chose to believe the stories about my father and blamed him for my misery, not realizing I used him as a scapegoat to cover my own creation

77

of turmoil and the absence of my mother. The rage I felt for my father was directed toward the loving people in my surroundings. That's how I came to express myself as an angry person, and how I justified my actions. In the process I was unaware of the hurt I caused either to others around me or to myself. Despite the loving care of my stepmother, Lorrie, who adopted me when my mother died, I missed the presence of my real mother, as I sensed her loving spirit was always near me. There was always the nagging feeling of abandonment I experienced. Despite knowing she was gone, I still fantasized that one day my mom would come and scoop me up, telling me she missed me like I did her. As a child I imagined sitting on her lap while she was telling me stories. When I was sad and cried myself to sleep, I visualized that she would hold me in her loving arms and dry my tears. I now know I was deeply wounded by the absence of my mother and her love and by the absence of a strong, supportive father. Only later in life did I learn the meaning of love from my own daughter, who finally thought me to love unconditionally, and from her father, my lover, who was only in my life for a short time. But let me tell you the rest of the story and the lessons of my journey."

We, the women of the cedar circle, settled in by the fire to be fully present in support of Maike's story. Around the circle appeared a 3-D picture showing us the story of her life.

Maike's Younger Years

As the scenery started to appear, we were drawn into the picturesque pagan community where Maike lived.

'Don't let her see it,' whispered the young maiden, who was preparing a gift for the celebration of my upcoming fourteenth birthday. I acted like I didn't know anything about the surprise party they had planned for me, but the behavior of our community gave away their plans. In the magical world I lived in, I was trained in the occult community to eventually become a priestess. Following in the footsteps of my stepmom, Lorrie, I found there was much to learn in the area of growing herbs, using the magic of healing, and connecting with spirit, but the most difficult thing to learn for me was the practice of unconditional love. The community I was brought up in was located off the beaten path where no regular folks would ever disturb us, except some local farmers who were too busy tending their farms to notice us. The people of the tribe were gentle and kind, the personal traits I had to work on most, because they didn't come naturally to me. My confused mind took me often to questioning where I came from. And with my upcoming fourteenth birthday, I couldn't help but think of my mother, who had given birth to me at the same age. I just couldn't imagine having a child at my age. I felt the trauma she must have gone through. I made a promise to myself that that kind of abuse would never happen to me. The stories the women in my community told me about my mother made her sound like the most beautiful person in the world with her gentle loving ways. I often daydreamed that she was still alive, but on the other hand I was relieved she wasn't, because I felt I could never live up to her goodness. *If only I would take more after my mom,* I often thought, *then all would be fine.* My father, however, was another case. I was troubled by the stories I heard about him. Apparently he was a brutal man who took advantage of other people without remorse, a harsh truth I was willing to believe. Even worse, I feared I was much like him. I knew that within my genes I carried my parents' traits, the innocent, loving, and intuitive talents of my mother on one side, which seemed to be hidden deep inside my cells and hard to get to, and the negative, addictive, and controlling mind of my father that lay just beneath the surface, showing up at random.

"I imagined that my intelligence was above that of other members of my tribe. As a child I could be very mischievous, bordering on being belligerent, using my aggression against others. There was not a speck of humility in my field. Sometimes I just couldn't help myself, as if I was invaded by demons that made me behave in an unfathomable, even mean, way. I would, mostly on purpose, sometimes hurt one of my tribe members. But even then, the people I lived with were so nice and loving that they forgave me and loved me just for who I was.

"My stepmom, the high priestess Lorrie, took a special interest in my training, treating me as the daughter she'd never had. Her wish was that I follow in her footsteps and become a high priestess. From the moment I was born, she had high expectations of me. The childless woman took me under her wing. I could do no wrong in the eyes of the leader of the community, which fact I used to my benefit. From the beginning I was placed on a pedestal. The gentle souls I lived with looked up to me for the daring, courageous behavior no one else would brave. Therefore I was able to wind everyone around my little finger, ruling the entire community. The one I knew as my mother worried that I would grow up a spoiled brat. She had a hard time watching me throw away my life and discard the teachings I'd received, seeing her dreams for me shattered in front of her eyes. The fact that I had a big personality and that everyone loved me made it difficult for her to discipline me. She must have felt she had created a monster who only thought of herself. It became clear I was not fit to be a priestess.

"As a young teenager, I struggled with hormonal imbalances. One moment I was down and depressed, and the next I was high and optimistic, a person for whom no mountain was too high to climb. The ups and downs were very noticeable to those who were in charge of teaching me. There was no way to prepare for my mood swings. I had hallucinations of spirits talking to me and was often plagued by nightmares. In some of my darkest moments, thoughts of suicide crossed my mind, a fear I never shared with others. In your time I would possibly have been diagnosed with bipolar disorder or another mental disorder."

Maike's Visits to Her Blood Family

"Throughout my young life, there were visits to the family of my mother, Ella. I remember how my grandmother would come to pick me up from our place in the woods and how we walked the long journey to her house, where I would stay for up to ten days at the most. My grandmother was very loving toward me, but there was also a deep sadness every time she looked into my eyes. Grandfather concentrated on his work most of the time. I remember the beautiful furniture he made. I was allowed to watch him sometimes when he carved flowers or birds into the wooden objects he worked on, transforming them into pieces of art. One time he made me a carved cross. When I would hold it just right in the light, the face of a woman appeared in the grain of the wood. I don't think he noticed it himself, but when I showed it to Grandmother, tears welled up in her eyes. She said, 'She looks just like your mama.' Some of my aunts and uncles had their own families and lived nearby. At their houses, I got to play with my little cousins when I was a young child. Four of the youngest of Mother's siblings still lived at home, but they had no interest in me. They worked hard during the day either outside with their dad or at the farmer's place next door. This was a totally different life from the one I had in my tribal community with its many spiritual disciplines. I soaked up the attention while I visited, and now and then my grandmother would tell me stories of my mother while I was sitting on her lap. And of course she made sure no one was around. She told me how my mother, at a very young age, loved nature and how she talked to and received messages from animals and the spirits of plants and trees. After I heard these stories I longed even more to be near my mother. My stepmother, Lorrie, was very loving toward me, but I never remember sitting on her lap. She was not as affectionate as my grandmother was. In secret I dreamed about walking with my real mother out in nature and communicating with the spirit world. I visualized her giving me advice when I needed it and knowing that I was always loved by her no matter what.

"My visits to my mother's family were complicated. The few times I went to town with Grandmother, people would stare at me with a strange glare in their eyes. Later I found out that the whole town knew what had happened to my mom and by whom she had been impregnated. That discovery resulted in the firing of my biological father, who was chased out of town. No one knew where he went after that. It seemed there were many more victims besides Mom.

"At one of my earlier visits, I noticed that one of my mother's sister's behavior toward me was off. Only because of my intuitive nature, I could feel the distance in my aunt's behavior directed at me. What I didn't understand was what influenced her demeanor when she was near me. I wanted to be liked so much, yet there was never enough time to get to know my family well. Was her behavior toward me because of the shame over what had happened to my mother, or was it because that looking at me would bring back memories she had of Mom that hurt her heart? At my young age, I could not discern the difference and I felt very insecure about it. That's how I made up the belief in my mind that my aunt didn't like me.

"When I got older, the visits with my family diminished from twice yearly to maybe once every two years. Now that my fourteenth birthday was approaching, I had lost contact with them completely. The only news we had heard, about a year prior, was that my grandmother was very sick, but that's all we knew. I felt abandoned again, longing to belong.

"Life went on in the small community in the countryside south of the city called London. By now I was eighteen years old. We would often visit other communities like ours a day or so journey's away, exchanging spiritual teachings. We even traveled to the sacred circle of stones called Stonehenge to perform a ceremony.

"I grew into a beautiful young woman, taking every opportunity to flirt with the opposite sex. I loved playing games of the heart with boys from the priesthood, messing with their minds. The elders of the community grew concerned about my behavior, even the high priestess Lorrie, who tried to see the light in me was disappointed with the choices I made in my life. I would be gone for days, sometimes weeks, in a row, letting no one know of my whereabouts. They had learned I stole the heart of a farmer's boy who wanted to marry me. When he proposed to me in front of his family, I shamed him. This drove the young man to almost commit suicide, but I had no remorse. I was untouched. I felt the desire to hurt the opposite sex for what they had done to my mother. That's how my immature mind worked. My heart was very cold.

"After the leaders of the community learned of the young lad's misery, my training for being a priestess was rescinded and I was sent away from the community to live in the big city of London. This was a shock to my entire system, as I'd never expected to lose the love the tribe tried so hard to give me. At that moment I was more appalled by their decision than sorry for my actions. In short, I didn't learn anything. The lesson was to come at a later time."

A New Life

"My new life in the city was not as easy as I had expected it to be, but soon I learned how to manipulate others. I found my way into higher social circles, being a charming lady of the night. I still struggled with my mental highs and lows, but I cleverly found the support I needed to cope with my mood swings. I had placed myself in dubious circles with people who were dark like me. Over the years I wised up a little and finally figured out that the people I hung out with would keep me in the dark, so I changed my demeanor toward people, which eventually landed me at the court of King George III. The king and his queen, Charlotte of Mecklenburg-Strelitz, took their roles of rulers of England very seriously. Such was not the case with the king's brothers, who, unlike the king, loved to party. I used the magic I had learned in my childhood community and took it to a whole new level to manipulate those at court. I was evenly loved by men as by women. The ladies liked my tips on beauty and my knowledge about how to make a man feel good and get what you want from him. I shared how to prevent being with child. And if an unwanted soul presented itself into a woman's womb, the woman would come to me to receive a magic potion to abort the fetus. I used my beauty and my magic powers to capture the guys' hearts, playing with their minds so they would fall madly in love with me. Once I had enough of them, I dumped them, leaving them brokenhearted. I made sure never to get too emotionally involved with anyone. Now and then the memories of my youth dwelt in my mind in the wee hours of the night. In those quiet moments I felt all alone, missing the love and support of the ones I had left behind at the community now so far away. I was aware of how I had missed out on receiving their love, something that was lacking at court. I became aware of the fact that I was bored and unhappy in this place where everyone faked their identity, including me. We were all playing roles, portraying a false image of ourselves. We had to stay on top of the game, you know. There was something missing in my life, something nagging in my gut. I realized I lived my life in accordance to the rules of the royal court, not in accordance with my soul's journey. Over time I slowly felt a pulling at my solar plexus and a heavy weight in my heart telling me something was off."

Finally, True Love

"One day, when I had the foolish belief that I was on top of my game, I literally walked into a man on the streets of London.

Immediately there was a connection between us two. I was falling hard for this man, and he for me. His energy filled the empty gap in my gut, which until meeting him had been filled with an old wound of sadness I couldn't describe. Besides falling deeply in love and having physical attraction for each other, we learned about our similar energies and training in the mysteries of the occult. Our romance had to stay secret, meeting whenever we could, because both of us had commitments elsewhere. I had never expected to fall in love, but this soul was like a gift from heaven. We were kindred spirits with equal knowledge of matters of magic. I felt he could read my mind, and his gentle, loving ways reminded me of my grandmother's loving arms and the childhood community I'd been raised in.

"My lover and I would meet as much as possible. Our love affair went on for more than a year. Of course at the royal court, they noticed my growing absence at the parties, since I was a favorite of many. Nevertheless I couldn't stay away from my lover, who stirred something deep inside me, something I'd never experienced before in my life. Was this feeling what my stepmother and the other members of my tribe had tried to teach me? It seemed like overnight I had changed from a selfish manipulator to a softer, gentler human being with compassion for others.

"The secret love affair lived on, our love continuing to grow. I felt I had blossomed like a rose in high season. It was tricky to lead a double life, but we did so, unable to get enough of each other's presence. It was like I had finally awakened to my true self and learned the lesson of what it's like to be vulnerable. For the first time in my life I felt emotions of love running through my veins. My chest was glowing with this soft, fluffy feeling that was difficult to describe. I was overcome with feelings of peace, joy, and happiness, which I'd never felt before.

"Then one day before my lover and I were to meet, I had this nagging feeling in my stomach that something was very wrong. When I showed up that afternoon at our secret place, I found the love of my life's dead body lying there with a knife in his chest, drenched in blood. Time stood still. I don't remember how I found the strength to leave his body there or how I arrived at court. All I knew to do at that moment was to go to my chamber. I found myself in a dark, empty place between the world of spiritual awakening with the love of my life, whom I considered to be my spiritual teacher, and the empty life at court with the fake smiles and lies the people told each other. After I put myself together and went back to court that night, I found myself noticing a strange energy hanging in the air. First I thought I was imagining the energy around me, thinking that my senses were not clear. For heaven's sakes, I had just lost the love of my life. I was numb. Later I found out that my lover had been killed by one of my jealous admirers at court. Everyone seemed to know about my not so secret love affair, and more mysteriously, everyone knew my lover had been killed. There was a conspiracy against me. Many in court felt it was payback time for the trail of ruination I had left behind. They were all against me, even those I had helped to get on top. My grief was unbearable. All I wanted to do was take my own life and set myself free to be with him; or go home and fall into the loving arms of my grandmother, though I didn't know if she was still alive; or be with my stepmother, Lorrie, living in the community in the woods outside of London—but I had burned all those bridges a long time ago.

"A couple of months later I noticed a change in my body. Intuitively I knew I was pregnant, and I knew instantly who the father was. Others in my environment were also aware of the fact I was with child. Soon the news traveled like a blazing fire, reaching the queen's chambers. The queen didn't know about my love affair. She was concerned that the child I was carrying had been fathered by one of her brothers-in-law. She took matters into her own hands and sent me away to her home country, Germany. I had to leave England without saying goodbye to my beloved stepmother and my childhood community. At that moment I knew, more than ever, the value of belonging. Up to that point, I had run away from the people who loved me and taken them for granted. My thoughts went back to my birth mother, thinking what it would have been like for her to be pregnant, to be cast away, and to be all alone in the world."

Alone in the World

"Grief-stricken, I arrived in a small town named Jemgum in the western part of Germany. I was placed in a convent for troubled women who, like me, would reside there until their babies were born. This convent was also used as a hospital for especially poor women. It was run by nuns who didn't know much about taking care of patients. Most of them cared selflessly for others from a deep well of doing service, but some of them also believed they gained God's blessings by providing good works, doing humane things for the poor."

"Time went by. A healthy daughter was born. I named her Trista. In the archives, her last name was listed as Prikker. No one knew why. The baby softened my character, as I was still grieving my loss. Being a new mother was one of the hardest things I had ever endured in my life. Now I was responsible for both of us, yet somehow my heart was full. Knowing the gift of the new life I had received from my lover gave me strength to go on. I felt as of his spirit was guiding me. Over time I found my place in the hospital among the nuns and was able to use my knowledge of herbal medicine."

Forgiveness

"Because of my past, I came to realize the trails of trouble I'd left behind would never be resolved if I didn't have remorse for what I had done. I learned that the power of forgiveness would transform my life. First I had to forgive myself for the horrible ways I treated others. I knew that which I had sown was coming back to me in a negative way, and would continue to do so until I changed the seeds I was planting. So I prayed and meditated, talking and listening to spirit, until I received the instruction to forgive myself first—and only then could I forgive others who had done me harm. The roles I played with the people of the community and at court were biting me in the butt. It was up to me to change. So I started the process of forgiving myself consciously, one day at a time, for all the harm I had done. Then I forgave those who had betrayed me in response to how I had treated them. It was a long and powerful process of transformation. To my surprise, spirit sent me an angel to work with in the form of a kind-spirited nun named Anna. She was the head of the women's hospital. Her knowledge of how the mind works and how we create energy in our life by the actions we take and the thoughts we think was way before her time. Anna had a big heart. It was not uncommon for her to hold someone's hand or let them cry on her shoulder. People felt comfortable in her presence and would open up to her, telling her about their troubled lives. She just had that effect on people.

Anna and I developed a deep connection, and together we took care of the women who would come to the hospital. She would address them with her wise and loving words, listen to their problems, and use the power of prayer to help them. I would use herbal medicine and perform magical healings with my hands. Together we became a powerful force in healing the body, mind, and spirit, yet no one knew what we were up to.

"Raising my daughter and receiving the loving guidance of Anna taught me compassion and unconditional love, the traits I struggled with in my early life. I finally understood what Lorrie and the community had been trying to teach me. My life had meaning now. I became a great teacher. I had the gift of growing herbs and using them to help people with their ailments, much like the high priestess Lorrie had done when my mother was sent to her. Behind the hospital a garden was dedicated to the growing of medicinal plants and herbs. For many years as the head herbalist, I would teach women how to grow herbs themselves to help their loved ones. The medicines were used in the hospital for healing the patients. The circle felt complete. With compassion, I dedicated myself to my child and to being of service to my community, especially women. What happened at the end of my life with my daughter and granddaughter is not my story to tell. It will be revealed in a later chapter."

Back at the Cedar Circle

When Maike was finished, we all sat in silence to process the story of her life. In her honor, we prayed and witnessed her amazing transformation, which transpired right in front of our eyes, like a movie shown on a screen. She was blessed to be sitting between her mother, Ella, and her daughter, Trista.

Lessons: Forgiveness, and Transformation from Dark to Light

After Maike finished sharing, Oma took the lead and showed us the lessons learned. "Maike," she said, "had the strength of an old soul who was able to express the dark side that lives in all of us. Her role was similar to the one Judas chose to play when he walked the earth with Jesus. He signed up to play that role prior to being born, and both he and Jesus knew what was to transpire. In a similar way, before Maike entered her life, she knew that the role she was to play was an opportunity to expose the darkness living within each of us. Her challenge was to overcome negative behavior. In her younger years, Maike made the choice to be persuaded by the negativity that was present in her field instead of embracing the loving energy of the community surrounding her. She is a great example for us all of how to heal and transform our ways when we are still alive in the physical. Her lessons changed all of our futures. With her unbalanced nature, she struggled, feeling torn between the ups and downs of her moods like a person who suffers from bipolar disorder and her false beliefs.

"At a young age she was exposed to the ways of the loving spiritual community and became aware of how different her behavior was. Her being sent away was actually a blessing and the beginning of her journey of healing. It took a while for the teachings to sink in, but eventually she understood on a deep level the harm she had done to those who loved her. At court she played her role as a trickster who would expose others to their dark side so they had an opportunity to change their ways if they so chose. The greatest lesson she learned was when she fell in love with an old soul who had been sent down to help her experience unconditional love. Through him she learned to look at herself in a different way, because her lover was like a mirror to her. With dedication and much work, she had the courage to travel deep within her psyche to look at the darkness of her soul and transform herself through forgiveness."

Guided Imagery: Forgiveness

After we heard Maike's story and Oma's teaching, we brought our attention back to the circle to perform a ceremony. We entered our sacred dream place, the circle of cedar trees standing strong in support of one another. The fire inside the circle was gently burning. I found my spirit joining those of the grandmothers.

It was Maike this time who asked for healing. The circle of grandmothers were well aware of her mischievous life, yet no one blamed or shamed her. They were loving toward her like always, because they knew she had played that role for all of us. "Let's get to work by releasing and letting go of this past life's trial," continued Oma. We all focused on getting centered in our spirit selves. Maike was at the center of our circle. The women started to clap and chant sacred songs. The sounds filled the air, surrounding us. Next to Maike's chair was a black box with ancient symbols on it. She went into a trance, her eyes rolling back. Oma continued to guide her, with the focus on releasing the guilt left in Maike's field. "This is a ceremony about forgiveness for all of us to process. First you, Maike, need to forgive yourself for the hurt you have caused others." We could see her darkness transforming into light when she affirmed, "I forgive myself for the pain I caused others and myself. I release these images from my genes and place them in the box." After she released the image, we witnessed her field bursting with light. Next, dark shimmering figures appeared in front of Maike. The first one was the essence of her father, in the form of a dark figure. We heard Maike talk to him in a strong voice. "I forgive you for your violent actions toward my mother and other women. I will release the energy I have created in mind about who you were, because it hurts only me. The image you represent as a violent rapist has no power and will be released from all women's blueprints from history to the present time." Then she placed the dark figure in the black box next to her and closed it. She continued to invite others into her circle, and one by one she forgave them and placed them in the box. With each act of forgiveness, her field shone brighter. When she was finished, she picked up the box and threw it in the fire, affirming her forgiveness. The flames of the fire first burst into dark red colors, creating black smoke, but soon the flames transformed into purple and blue colors. For a split second, Saint Germaine appeared in the dancing purple flames, and then disappeared. We all felt our energy fields changed. Throughout the circle our lights shone as one purple blaze.

I awoke from my meditation in my favorite meditation place. The soft music was still playing. My energy field felt cleansed and rejuvenated. I was grateful for the gift Maike had given us all.

She fought the battles within herself between darkness and light, good and bad, attributes that live in all of us. Her message for us is to release the emotions and false beliefs so we can let go of the generational wounds that bind us in a negative way and become free to be part of the new evolution that is in front of us. This illustrated the fact that when we hold a grudge toward others, we only hurt ourselves, because others will never know how we feel toward them.

Getting to know where we came from and acknowledging that our ancestors' adversities are still alive in our DNA will make room for an opportunity to let go of these old energies, unlock new doors, and heal. God has a plan for all of us. It is up to us to listen and walk through that door. There is a new wave of light in the air all over the world, replacing the old energies with new streams of compassion, love, and acceptance for each other. That is what Maike demonstrated in her life!

Chapter 8

Murder of a Healer

Trijntje Prikker, Born 1799 in Jemgum, Germany

The Industrial Revolution

Trista was born in the middle of the Industrial Revolution, which gave birth to the scientific studies that popped up all over Europe. With the earlier invention of the microscope in 1590, scientists were now able to look at the cells of the body and discover the microorganisms—viruses and bacteria—that we now know to be the main cause of infectious diseases. It was during this time that the discovery of modern medicine developed. With research in chemistry, genetics, and laboratory technology, and the study of the body's anatomy and physiology, many new ideas came into play in the field of medicine.

This knowledge of microorganisms led scientists to look at how germs—bacteria and viruses—enter the body. It was discovered that many contagious diseases could be prevented by the simple act of washing hands. Florence Nightingale, who instigated the importance of washing hands and taking other sanitary measures when cleaning wounds, became the ringleader of a new movement.

In religious circles prior to this time, a serious illness was seen as a result of sin, and getting sick was considered to be a punishment from God. On the other hand, the old pagan belief of disease was that it was the result of an invasion of negative spirits or demons that needed to be released through ritual by a shaman, priest, or witch. In the past, simple diseases were taken care of by mainly the grandmothers, who treated their families with herbal teas, vegetable and herbal stews, and poultices made from plants (for skin diseases).

Some five thousand years ago, the Chinese looked at diseases as an imbalance that could be a result of diet, emotions, or spiritual or environmental disharmonies. They used their herbal medicinal formulas and even acupuncture in accordance to the seasons and the positions of the stars. Herbs were planted and harvested at just the right time so they would have the ultimate effect.

Now, with new discoveries in modern medicine, old folklore ways of healing were set aside, making room for chemical-based medicine created in the lab and the ability to look inside the cells of the body in order to diagnose more precisely.

It was amid that environment that Trista grew up. Knowledge of herbal medicine was still well used in the rustic areas of Europe where modern medicine was not yet available for the common folk. It was this way in Jemgum, the small village where Trista was born, in the monastery of the women's hospital, where people still relied on the old ways of healing. The hospital ward was directed by women only, mainly nuns who had no knowledge of medicine and who knew little about herbal remedies, but who believed strongly in the power of prayer, with the exception of Anna and Maike who helped many people and who later became Trista's mentors.

Wisdom At The Cedar Grove

A delicious aroma filled the air, coming from the cauldron hanging above the fire. The women of our circle of ancestors had created this sacred food together by harvesting vegetables, herbs, and roots from the woods and the nearby community garden. Most of them have had lifetimes of combined knowledge in healing. Long ago, it was the women, and especially the grandmothers, of families who would use their knowledge of curing common illnesses with simple vegetables and herbs like mint, garlic, and onion for conditions related to the lungs; vegetables or herbs such as rosemary, basil, and oregano for digestive problems; and the leaves of plantain and the flower of marigold to ease skin disorders. Only when a serious illness presented itself was a woman healer called upon, who many times was consigned to live on the outskirts of the village because people feared her magical powers.

The stew was dished up for all of us to enjoy and was blessed with a short prayer. In silence we ate, as was the protocol of pagan tradition. When eating in silence, the focus is on the nutrition of the food eaten and the gratitude one has for receiving such gifts from Mother Earth. After our meal we gathered around the fire for sharing the amazing stories of our ancestors' lives. Today the third ancestor in line would share the story of her life.

Trista's Story

Trista, the daughter of Maike, had the floor today.

"I'm gladly telling my story because I feel the lifetime lived as Trista was one of the best lives I ever had. Despite the trauma, I was able to do the things I was sent out to do. Individually we all have had many lifetimes, and each lifetime has one story, but at the end they all run together; we all are part of each other's tales. In the first place, the purpose of telling the stories is so we can share our lessons with those alive today. It is our wish that women worldwide will find healing when we invite them to our circle, so we all can support each other and gain a better understanding of the fact that we are not alone in the world. And second, we create an opportunity to release the emotions of stored experiences from the genes of those still alive today and free the gene pool for future descendants. From here we begin a new journey with a clean slate.

"I was called weird by my young friends, because they didn't understand I was seeing things only a gifted child could see. For this I felt privileged, as I was surrounded by amazing people and I came from a line of healers. Both of my parents were gifted with the knowledge of healing. My mother knew about herbal medicine, and my father, whom I never knew, was blessed with psychic abilities. As the daughter of Maike, I showed much potential. All I had to do was to stay on the right path. I guess you could give my mother credit for sharing her own mistakes, which she terribly regretted later on in life.

"In my young life I was surrounded by other women and maidens practicing and learning the pagan ways of ceremony and healing. We lived in a small community of like-minded people far enough from the village to be safe. We were neither well received nor understood by the Christians of the surrounding communities. Consequently we were left alone. Our gardens were planted and harvested in accordance with the face of the moon, the stars, and the seasons. From early in my life you could find me in the woods and gardens talking to my magic friends, as I called them, who taught me the secrets of the earth. I claimed that I remembered important information about times before I had been born. Even within the pagan community, my unorthodox ways could be misunderstood, but because I was well-liked, they left me alone.

"When I reached adulthood, I became one of those healers who lives at the edge of town. From the rafters in my cabin, herbs and roots were hung to dry, making my home smell kind of musky. The nearby townspeople consulted me about herbal medicine when an illness became serious. Every week I would travel into town to sell my ointments, decoctions, and herbal teas at the local market. I was noticed by the townsfolk, who didn't see any threat in my being there.

"One day I was called in to meet with the priest of the church. I knew him from passing by when I did volunteer work at the women's hospital. He was visiting the sick and praying for them. He asked me if I was willing to help a well-respected citizen who was critically ill, saying that only a miracle could save this man. They had tried many of the modern medicines to no avail. So I went to work on him, using my gifts to save the man from dying. Soon I was the talk of the town.

"Months later I was surprised by a visit from the priest. I offered him a cup of tea. When I asked the reason for his visit, I learned there was some concern among the folks from town about how I used my gift to heal. They had said it was ungodly the way I had saved the man from dying. In their eyes, only God could grant such a healing. The priest ensured me he was not in agreement with the others, saying that he had come to warn me to be careful and not to sell my herbs at the weekly market until the excitement had died down. I noticed the two of us had much in common despite the difference in our beliefs in God.

"I stopped going to the markets, but people still paid me visits when in need of healing. One of these visitors was the priest, who came in to consult me about a stubborn skin rash. Before he left, I asked him to think about who or what was getting under his skin lately to determine if it had something to do with his skin breakout. On his next visit, his skin was much better. He shared with me that my question had made him think about what was bothering him. He was very nervous, and it took him a long time to come forth with his discovery, but he finally shared with me that the rash had started when people spoke ill of me for my healing abilities. He was pained by their harsh words, more so because he had all sorts of feelings for me that he didn't understand.

"The words were out now. I knew he had carefully thought about it for a long time and finally had gained the courage to tell me how he felt about me. My cheeks turned red. I also had noticed how comfortable I was in his presence. There were no words to describe how I felt. We embraced, holding on to each other, sharing our love. The priest became a regular visitor at the little cabin. Our love had to be kept in secret, out of fear of how his flock would respond. Of course we couldn't keep our blossoming romance a secret. There was talk that I, the healer, had placed a spell on the priest to control him. The congregants pressured the priest to turn his back on me. When I told him I was pregnant with our child, he pleaded with me to be converted to Christianity to save my soul. 'How could I betray my ways and beliefs?' was my response. It was too much to ask. I wouldn't be myself anymore. It would mean that I could not practice my healing ways or search for roots in the woods. And what about our child? How would this new soul be raised? We both felt devastated and concerned for our child.

"In order to save me, the priest preached from the pulpit to his flock to have tolerance for fellow citizens, even if their beliefs were different, and asked the congregation to pray for my soul. I decided to leave the town and go stay with the pagan community some distance away, close to my mother, until the baby was born. It was there I gave birth to a healthy baby girl I named Alida.

"After I regained my strength, I went back with my child to my cabin. A couple of days later, when I was settled in for the night with my baby within my sight, I entered a deep sleep. Once I woke up after hearing loud banging at the door, some visitors entered my cabin and dragged me outside into the darkness, where they beat me to death. One of the maidens from the pagan community who stopped by for a visit the next morning heard the cries of the baby and discovered my body drenched in blood not far from the cabin."

A Look from Above

"The night of my murder, I awoke to the disturbing sound of someone banging at the door. I thought this person must be in deep distress, so I hustled to open the door to see who it was that needed help. Soon three men with covered faces burst in and dragged me outside, calling me names. Next I felt beatings on my head with a blunt object, followed by a sharp pain in my chest. Then I lost consciousness and drifted up above my body. ... Looking down, I noticed one of the men watching over my body, spitting on what was left of me, before the three of them ran off. Confused in this state, I drifted inside to check on my baby, who was, thank God, sound asleep. I tried to scream, but no sound came out of me. In a confused state, I hovered over the scene. I wanted so bad to go down and hold my baby to my chest, but I was limited by the lightness of my spirit body. Gravity wouldn't allow me to descend. Out of fear of what would happen to my child, I thought of the only thing I could: to alarm my mother. I found my spirit drifting to her, trying to get her attention. I could see her waking up thinking she'd had a bad dream about me being killed. Thinking that something like this could not happen to her loved ones, she went back asleep. Later that night she was somewhat alarmed remembering the dream, but she dismissed her fear, deciding to take action early the next morning. She asked one of the maidens to leave early in the morning and travel by my place to check on me, just to be sure. From above, I felt relieved that help would come soon for my child and she wouldn't have to die alone without me.

"I kept watch all night over the babe. Whenever she woke up, I could comfort her, as she could see and hear me.

"When the maiden, arrived she found my lifeless body lying outside. Then she took the baby and rushed her to my mother. It was now time for my spirit to go; my child was safe. My spirit drifted up and moved to the light, where I was welcomed by beautiful beings.

"The father of my child was devastated when he heard the news; he had not yet seen me or the baby since our return. He fell into deep despair, which prevented him to do his work. He was accused by the townspeople of having had an affair with me and was sent away. Thank God the pagan community took care of him and our child. He was confused about where he belonged and even more disturbed about his spiritual beliefs. Could he go back and be a priest? Would he be accepted with his previous record?

"After he was stable enough, he took the babe with him to his birthplace, Slochteren, a town a day or so journey's away on the other side of the border in Groningen, a province in the Netherlands. The new grandmother Maike and the pagan community were devastated to see them go. Maike had pleaded with him to leave the child behind and let her raise her, but he didn't want to hear her plea, as he was determined to take the babe to his family."

Lesson: Listen to the Small Voice Within

I was sobbing at the circle in the presence of my women ancestors. The story of Trista touched a chord inside me. It was as if the cells of my body remembered the brutality of how I and many women had been killed in the history of the world for doing the work of God. I was truly shaking and was surprised how calm and loving the women in the circle were. Then I was reminded of the fact that they don't experience emotions like we do here on earth; all they know is love. The purpose for which I was here was to listen and observe and to bring forth healing to those who are at this moment on the planet in the physical.

Trista continued, saying that the need to show those living upon the earth that it is to let go to make way for the shift of awakening of humanity is upon us. So many past emotions are still stored in the physical; the body is the densest it has ever been in human history. Therefore it's time to release the old stories of suffering, which don't serve anyone.

"We on this side of the veil," continued Trista, "are not affected in any way by these past emotions. We all have had many, many lifetimes where we played the role of either victim or victimizer, and we view these experiences as being part of the evolution of humanity, things that served the job of eventually bringing back compassion. And here we are, all of us, whether in the physical or spiritual, with the same goal of entering a new era of love, compassion, and peace. It's time to let go of the past, awaken to the new energy that is evolving, and move forward."

"But how can we let go?" was my question. "We are so entangled in our old patterns and beliefs that tell us life is suffering that we become victim of those patterns and beliefs."

"It is that victimhood that keeps people from moving forward. Some people are addicted to their negative beliefs. It somehow serves them. And they can use such a belief to their own benefit, especially when they get attention for being the victim. Why would you give that up?

"It is of the utmost importance to develop a positive-thinking mind. Of course that takes a lot of practice and dedication and is the hardest thing to do. Many already have mastered this new awareness through prayer and meditation. These are the best tools to connect with your spirit mind and to listen to that small voice within. Everyone can do this. All that is needed is time and the aspiration to make a change.

"Just remember, humanity is well on its way toward awareness. We have never been here before in the history of humankind. The shift is real, and we on this side are very excited for the new wave of positive energy making an entrance in the minds of all people."

Guided Imagery: Honoring the Healer

As we gathered in the woods, our circle felt heavy after listening to Trista's story. "My story," continued Trista, "is what happened to healers throughout history. And things were sometimes even worse. Many healers were burned at the stake, and others were stoned to death." Each woman in the circle had made prayer flags to be used in a ceremony of praying to the highest spirits. Candles were lit and incense was burned, all with the focus of releasing negative beliefs and patterns created over time, and especially letting go of the devastating experiences women healers had to endure. The intent of the circle was to free the memory cells stored in our DNA, the things holding these images, and to transform them, thereby empowering the female species.

We all relaxed and prayed, which led us into deep meditation. "Today we are guided to honor the healers of the world." A wave of women healers entered our circle. There must have been thousands of them present. A sacred high priestess appeared out of thin air in our midst. She was dressed in a luminous robe reflecting the world and the universe. In her left hand she held a golden staff decorated with sacred symbols. In the palm of her right hand she held a silver globe decorated with jewels and golden lines representing the grids of the earth. "All of you who are present here have been murdered for doing the sacred work of healing. The globe in my hand reflects the work you have done on earth and the sacredness of your holy being." The globe in her hand lit up, releasing thousands of beams of light. Then the light moved through the circle, touching every healer's forehead. "The residue still present in the memory cells of those living today will be released as of now." Next the lights from the high priestess and all the healers burst from the circle and found their way to the earth, finding all those still plagued by the memory imprinted in their genes and releasing them.

We emerged from a deep trance, waking from the amazing scene just played out before our eyes. When I checked in with my physical body, I could feel how the light had changed me. "Remember who you are," sounded the voice of the high priestess. "Your healing work is needed in the world. Don't be afraid. From now on you will be protected; you will never be killed again for being a healer." Then she disappeared. I awoke to find myself relaxed and free.

Chapter 9

Misuse of Priestly Power

Alida de Vries, Born 1827 in Germany

Setting the Mood

I followed my regular routine of writing, first I went to my favorite place, a cedar building in my backyard, where I knew I would find peace and no one would disturb me. Like other times, I lit candles and incense to get in the mood. Then I slowly started breathing in and out. With the rhythm of the tones of the soft music playing in the background, I felt my mind and body relax. Soon I found myself in a state of deep meditation where I connected with my subconscious mind. I suddenly pictured myself walking in the woods toward the cedar grove. The grandmothers welcomed me with their warm smiles; it was as if I had never left.

The next ancestor was ready to tell her story of her experience of having lived the life of Alie. Like the others, she was telling the story from her spiritual self, having a bird's-eye view on her life but with a different perspective. Her appearance was exquisite, with long dark hair and azure-blue eyes. Her softly spoken words echoed through the circle. We were all in awe watching her, listening to the powerful declaration of her life.

Alie's Story

"I was born in the midst of a traumatic event I of course had no knowledge of. Soon thereafter, I was taken back by my father, who was a priest, to the pagan community where I was born not long before. After we arrived, my grandmother Maike took charge of caring for Father and me. My father was in shock and in need of extra healing and rest. The pagan community was afraid for his well-being since his demeanor was one of despair. He wouldn't eat or speak. All he did was stare out into deep space, being in his own dark world. I as a baby of course had no knowledge of what had happened to my parents in my young life. I would learn the story of the beginning of my life much later.

"Months of recovery were needed before my dad was somewhat better. After that period he decided to take me to his family. Grandmother Maike, a leader in the pagan church, was devastated to see the only connection she had left to her daughter leave. She herself was still grieving from the loss she had endured. Fear that she would never see me again, and with a heavy heart, she said goodbye to us. The only light in this dark period was that she felt relieved to have gotten to know the man who loved her daughter so much and the child whom she'd helped bring into the world. Pieter the priest had a gentle soul. She was convinced he would take good care of his own daughter. Of course, Grandma Maike didn't know that I, Alie, was to be brought up by my paternal grandmother. Nor did she suspect that my other grandmother, Neeltje, would forbid any contact between her and me. And so we parted ways and she said her farewell with a broken heart and tears in her eyes."

Alie's Paternal Grandmother

"After a couple of days traveling, with me now being seven months old, my father and I arrived in Sappemeer, his birthplace. On arrival at his parents' house, he proudly introduced me to his family. However, the welcome was less than pleasant. Pieter's mother, my new oma, was coldhearted about meeting me—a welcome my father had not been prepared to come home to. Instead of encountering a warm homecoming, he was criticized for his love affair with my mother, who practiced witchcraft and thus was evil in the eyes of his family. He must have been hypnotized by her, was his mother's remark, and how dare he bring a child home who came from the loins of such a woman? Didn't he realize the trouble God would place on their family? She feared the worst. After she was asked to raise the child, she replied that she would raise her with a stern hand. If her granddaughter showed any sign of magic or witchcraft, she would beat it out of her, he could be sure of that.

"After the harsh welcome, Pieter fell into an even deeper depression. Soon after his arrival home, he left, hoping to move as far away as he could so as not to be reminded of the trauma he'd endured of losing the love of his life and of the vicious harsh words spoken to him by his mother. He had regrets for having taken the baby away from her other grandmother, who showed so much love for the child, but it was too late to return. He knew there was no way for him to raise his daughter by himself, so the best thing to do was to leave her in the care of his mother.

"And so I, Alie, started my young life in an inharmonious household. At a young age, I was starved for love and attention, something I didn't receive in the harsh Dutch household. Over time my oma softened her heart a little toward me. The only subject she would not diverge from was religion. She would make sure I would grow up with the fear of God in me like she herself had. The relationship between my grandmother and me fortunately grew a little closer when my opa died. I was only four at the time. It was now only the two of us left. She had no one else in her life to rely on. I didn't miss my opa much, since he had not played a big part in my life. He'd worked most of the time, and when he was home, he was quiet like a mouse, lost in his Bible or another book.

"One of the first memories I have is of something that happened at a very young age. I saw mystifying lights dancing in the dark at night. I must have been four or five years old. In my dreams I was visited by a beautiful lady who became my best friend and confident. Somehow I knew not to talk about my experiences to Oma or others. One day when I asked Oma where my parents were, she grew pale and fell deathly silent. It was as if ice-cold air permeated the space between us. After that incident, I never again had the courage to ask about where I had come from. In silence I dreamed I was a princess and that one day, once they realized I was alive, my parents would pick me up and take me to their castle.

"When I was five years old, we were visited by a lovely woman from the east. The woman looked at me with familiar eyes. For a second I thought I recognized something in her. I felt a strange connection between us, like I had seen those eyes before. I was sent away so the two women could talk. After my return, I found both women with tears in their eyes, like they were hiding a painful mysterious secret I was not to know about. I knew it had something to do with me, but I didn't dare ask any questions. This was not the royal connection I had dreamed of. When the mysterious woman finally left, I felt a profound tugging in my stomach unfamiliar to me up until that time. I didn't know what to do with these feelings.

"In the future, Oma and I would be visited by this lady more often. When she came, I always noticed a feeling of love previously unknown to me. After the lady's visit, Oma's behavior often changed, like she was afraid and insecure.

"Although my oma's demeanor toward me had mellowed over the years, she was still very stern in her religious beliefs. There wasn't a whole lot of flexibility in the way she thought. It was as if she was holding many dark secrets. Throughout my youth, there were daily visits to church and constant prayers. I went to religious classes every day and spent a lot of time at the orphanage behind the church, where Oma left me often. The kids who lived there all looked sick and depressed; it wasn't unusual to see a child beaten by one of the nuns. After I witnessed one of those beatings, I felt blessed to be living with my oma. She did the best she could under the circumstances, but I felt often suffocated as a child because of the strict rules I had to follow. Then on one of those days while I was at church, at the age of eight years old, the abuse started ..."

Misuse of Priestly Power

"The priest had his eye on me, probably thinking this innocent child would be an easy target. He started grooming me at first with sweet soft words, telling me how special I was and saying that the games we played were to be our little secret. Next he started threatening me, saying that if I were to tell anyone, there would be great consequences. Over time the abuse got worse. I didn't dare tell my oma out of fear of the threat placed upon me that she would die if I told. My abuser groomed me with his sick mind, telling me it was God's will that he treat me this way. Of course I didn't know anything about what was happening, but I knew something was terribly wrong. The abuse went on for over a year, but I didn't know what was happening. I had no language to explain it.

"Because I couldn't tell my oma, out of fear what would happen, I started praying to Mother Mary, whose picture at church with the baby Jesus on her lap had made a great impression on me, even more so than the image of Christ on the cross. I felt he didn't belong on that cross and thought it was cruel that people left him hanging there on that cross for all these years. I couldn't understand that. I felt he needed help, so it was safer for me to pray to his mother. Besides praying to Mother Mary, I also prayed to the kind woman visiting our house. She inspired me with her gentle manners. It was as if she knew me, inside and out. I hadn't seen her for months now. My only hope was she would be visiting soon. Somehow I felt safe to pray to her. In my prayers I expressed the hope that things would change for the better.

"Not long after, the mysterious woman came for a visit. When I arrived at home, I found Oma and the lady talking. I felt somewhat safe in the lady's presence, and I wished that somehow I could talk to her about my grim situation. What I didn't know, of course, was that this woman had the ability to see things that were unknown to most, a trait I later learned my mother had also.

"When I entered the room, the lady looked at me with friendly observing eyes. They looked deep into my soul. It was as if she knew what I had gone through. After the strange woman had visited us and left, I knew something had changed in my grandmother. She was distraught, it seemed, and she looked ashen. No words were spoken between us. Oma's behavior was ice-cold. At first she looked at me with blank sad eyes, and then she gave me a hug, telling me everything would be fine. I didn't know what had just happened. She'd never hugged me before.

"Over the next few days life changed drastically for me. I felt a tremendous relief when I learned the priest had left. Some of the church people glared at me with peculiar looks in their eyes, yet no one talked to me about anything. A while later when I was praying to thank God for saving me from this evil man, I felt the presence of the mysterious lady entering my space. Then I remembered having asked the lady for help in my prayers. Would God have worked through the lady and Mother Mary? Had the lady been sent to me by God to save me? All these questions crossed my mind, but no one would be able to answer them for me. I trusted that God was with me always and that whatever happened in my life, he was there and would send someone to help me. Not long after this, the lady returned for another visit.

"Prior to her visit, I had noticed the fact that Oma's energy was nervous, as it had been for a couple of days now. I had no idea what was wrong with her, but I was concerned. I was now approaching my tenth birthday. It was early afternoon when the mysterious lady knocked on our door. The two women first sent me out to get eggs from the neighbors, but when I came back, they were waiting for me and gestured for me to sit down. I was shaken to the core of my being. With trembling knees, I could hardly compose myself, due to my uncontrollable fear of what lay ahead. The lady introduced herself as my other oma, Maike, the mother of my mom. I was so excited to hear the news that I flew into her arms, but right away I composed myself, being aware of my other oma's presence.

"I finally learned about the story of my mother being murdered and my father leaving me behind. Now I realized why my new oma had felt so familiar to me and why I was comfortable in her presence. She was family and she had always loved me. For the first time in my life I was talked to as if I mattered. I learned how much the two women had suffered from losing their children. Throughout the evening we laughed and cried, and it was decided I would go for a couple of months each year to my oma Maike, who lived some way to the east in a little town in Germany."

Alie's Visits to Germany

"My whole world changed when I went for visits to Germany. I never knew how different others could be in their belief in God. The community Oma Maike belonged to was worshipping in a totally different way than what I was used to at home, in light of the strict rules of our church. It was hard to adjust to at first. I felt kind of guilty when I observed the way they talked to spirit and how they felt accepted by God, a far cry from the guilt that was ingrained in me at our church, but eventually I adapted to their ways. I learned to see God in whatever is around me, be it in a person, a tree, or an animal. The members treated each other with love and respect.

"I learned about herbal medicine. The community members took me out into nature early in the morning to pick a certain plant for healing. The morning dew was still hanging on the leaves. They told me that's where the real magic is, in these drops of sacred water. I also liked the way they prayed for people. It was more like writing an affirmation of what they wanted the healing to be like and a visualization of how that would turn out, instead of asking permission from a higher power and hoping you deserved to be healed. It was all very heartwarming.

"What I really liked about their worship was how it made them happy and smile. Their rituals were filled with singing, dancing, and laughter, and there was always good food to share. Despite how much I liked the newfound energy in the country to the east, I somehow felt guilty about my oma at home and felt responsible for being with her."

Lesson: God Is Everywhere

"Eventually I grew up to be a content young woman. I married at a young age, raising a family of my own and working in my garden growing foods for our family. Besides the garden, we always had a couple of goats that gave us the luxury of making goat cheese and sharing goat milk with the young mothers who had difficulty breastfeeding their babies. All in all we had a good life. From my childhood I took with me the imprints of the sacred ceremonies I had experienced during my visits to Germany. For the rest of my life I kept an altar in my home, where I would pray every day for people who were sick and those who were less fortunate. A picture of Mother Mary was always present on the altar, and there were always candles burning for my parents and my two omas, I prayed for their spirits to be healed. I kept close to the church. My mission was to use my intuition to spot those who were in need of care, especially the children of the community. Blending the two spiritual traditions worked well for me. I was able to recognize how the rules of the church were based on fear. My oma and many others had fallen victim to that. Despite this, I always found God's presence in the building of the church—but not always in the people.

"I never knew much about my father. He was never to return. Maybe he was no longer alive. No one knew where he was, not even his mother. I felt she kept his whereabouts a secret from me because of her inability to express the grief she suffered from losing her son. My father, who abandoned me at such a young age, never showed up in my life again after he left me in the care of his mother. The only thing I learned from his mother was that my father was a man of God. She was very proud of that, but his name was too painful for her to mention. Long after Oma passed, I found out what happened to my father. Sadly, she died without ever hearing from him. A visitor came to town telling the story that my dad had died a long time ago at a monastery in the south of the country. Soon after he had left his family, he contracted a mysterious disease and wasted away till he died, without ever writing home."

Alie finished her life story and then told us to trust the intuition we have as women, because all of us come from a line of healers and seers. Despite the strict rules of the church, I had still been blessed to find God there. God is not a religious being, but is to be found in every church and every gathering in his name. And Christ was not a Christian. But the spirits of the Father and the Son still show up in our lives in mysterious ways. The other important lesson learned was that no matter where your religion takes you, we are all children of God. No one is exempt.

Guided Imagery: Mother Mary, Releasing Abuse

After Alie had spoken, we all sat in silence for a while in the circle by the fire, taking in her powerful story. Finally she spoke again. "If it hadn't been for the trust I had in God, I probably would not have survived my abuse. There are still so many boys and girls enduring similar abuse in the world today. Let us all pray for them, and let them feel our love and support from spirit the way I felt it." We could see the darkness leave her body and enter the fire. Then a healing green light moved into her heart chakra. From there it was transported as healing light and moved into all the cells of her body. I could feel the same energy entering my physical body. I visualized my memory cells being cleansed from her experience for all future generations. The light then traveled to all children and adults alive on earth today who have suffered abuse. We could see how many received the energy of healing in their heart. Now they had a way to let go and change their lives. With a little luck, they might transform their victimhood into empowerment.

We continued in prayer, when suddenly the wind picked up and rushed through the giant cedar trees, a sign of spirit introducing itself at the ceremony of our women's circle. All of a sudden a female figure appeared in a shimmering blue light. In a soft voice she introduced herself as the spirit of Mother Mary. She told us that she had heard Alie's prayers as a child in need. Next to emerge from our own circle was Alie's mother, Trista, who appeared amid brightly colored golden lights. "I was the one who paid you visits when you were a child," she said to Alie. "You would see my energy as mystifying lights." At that moment Alie lost it and ran to hug the two women. The angelic voice of Mary continued teaching us that all humans hold the light within. She said, "Those who have suffered are touched by the Holy Spirit." She then suggested that we women center ourselves, close our eyes, and feel the touch of spirit upon us. I felt a wave of energy moving through me. "My wish is," she continued, "that everyone who listens to or reads these words will feel the same blessing you all feel at this circle." Turning to Alie, she said, "Let's not forget your grandmother who raised you. There is no time in the realm of spirit, because everything happens all at once." After she had given her blessing, the essence of Mary disappeared. Her presence left a holy imprint on all of us in the circle. When I awoke from my meditation, I felt I had to pinch myself, because this experience was unbelievably powerful. It was magical beyond belief.

For all who seek the light of healing, these blessings are for you to receive. You are no different from I. Remember, you are the light this world needs. You are loved!

Chapter 10

Domestic Violence

Trijntje Bandsma, 1863–1943, Born in Sappemeer, Groningen

Sharing Our Stories

I was excited to again find myself at the circle of the cedar grove where my grandmothers gathered in spirit. When I looked around, I realized how honored I felt to be chosen as the one to tell my ancestors' tales. Every woman present was glowing in a luminous light that radiated through the entire circle. When I looked at my own spirit's reflection, I noticed that it was glowing as well. There is no separation here on the other side; we are all one in spirit, part of the universal flow. The crackling of the fire added to the mysterious atmosphere I had come to know so well during my visits. A soft wind caressed the cedar trees, swaying the branches back and forth. Birds were singing as if they wanted us to know they were there to serenade us in support. It felt like the spirits of nature blending with our circle of ancestors. Oma took the lead. She was holding a talking stick, an indication that all should honor the one who speaks and refrain from interrupting the flow of her story. We all listened with great respect and compassion.

"We are approaching the final level of our genetic cleansing," Oma said. "We represent all grandmothers. This cleansing will weave a common thread from our past lives to the lives of our next line of family members. By sharing our stories, we give permission to the ones alive today to let go of old outdated rules that are not working and will not work for the new members of the next seven generations. From this moment forward, now that we have cleansed, decoded, and renewed the information we hold in our DNA, the human field will become less dense. Like we said before, we on this side of the veil are not affected by our experiences anymore. Our goal is to help you, the reader, when you visit this sacred circle, to release the old, to heal, and to become the person you were born to be. All we want to do now is to remove and clear old ways and resolve the negative vibes still present in the genetic makeup of our descendants."

It was Tressa's turn to tell her story today. Tressa is the mother of my oma, my great-grandmother whom I never met. All that I can remember of her is seeing a picture of her in which she is sitting on a front porch peeling potatoes with a big colander on her lap and with a pan filled with water next to her on the porch to place the peeled and cut potatoes in.

Tressa's Story

"I was born in the late summer of 1863, the firstborn of twin girls. We received the names of Trijntje and Wassina. I always thought they had switched our names, as I never liked mine. That's why I was thrilled to use the name Tressa. As twins we were not particularly close growing up. That was to come later, when we both were adults and married. I was brought up in a loving family. My father was a carpenter, and Mother kept a garden, raised chickens, and tended goats. There was harmony in our family. I did feel I had a special relationship with my mother; we shared the gift of loving nature and the love of growing a garden. Her experience as a child in the church and later within the pagan community shaped her spiritual beliefs. This led her to a greater understanding of who God was in her eyes, a concept she shared with me only because I was curious about the subject. I learned that one can find God anywhere, in both pagan religions and church religions. Although both have flaws, they still have a sacred aspect to them, namely, the presence of the Holy Spirit. It just depends on how a person interprets it for themselves. What I liked about the pagan beliefs was the idea of seeing God or the Goddess in every living thing, no matter if it was a person, a tree, an animal, or even the earth. The pagans would honor every way of life that carried the life force. They communicated with the spirits of nature and therefore learned how herbs, trees, vegetables, and even animals could help with human ailments. What I liked about the Christian church, on the other hand, was that they honored a woman, Mother Mary. And the stories of Jesus intrigued me, like when he said that all humans are able to do the things he did, and even greater things than that. I felt he spoke directly to me. I myself loved to go to church and feel the energy of the Holy Spirit talking to me. That's how my belief was formed.

"Because of Mom's role in church as the one who got things done, people somehow flocked to her and told her all their problems. That was also the reason the townspeople hired Dad as a carpenter. They loved to come by our place to buy goat's milk and eggs from Mother, and in the summer fresh vegetables and flowers. People somehow wanted to be near her. I enjoyed growing all the different crops with her and felt the earth energized me whenever I stuck my hands in the dirt and talked to the little imaginary divas. In late summer we would can vegetables and dry the herbs to get us through the cold winter months.

"As Tressa, I show you my energy field at that time. See how it resembled a bird with broken wings?" We watched as she dropped her shoulders. Her black-sleeved left arm seemed to hang limp. "That's how I felt as an adult woman who silently suffered in a violent relationship. I felt that my hands were tied and I had no voice. I didn't inherit any of the spiritual life skills my ancestors carried in their bloodline, or so I thought, but I know now the reasons why I was not able to have access to my higher spirit.

"The time of linear thinking and technology was upon us. Each woman living at that time unknowingly played an important role for future generations, as we learned in later times. Women held the sacred love in their heart that was the glue that kept the family together, while the men were introduced to the logical mind of thinking. Our husbands' jobs changed from working the fields and using their hands to standing at a conveyer belt at one of the new factories. This did a number on some of the men, who were not used to be confined in a closed-off space for long hours each day, doing the same work day in and day out. We were all in it together, and our spirits knew before we entered this lifetime that we were playing the role that would not be understood until much later, the role of how the left brain versus the right brain was valued. Of course we didn't know we had chosen these roles prior to our birth. You who live in this present time reap the fruits of our labors. Now the creativity and intuition of the female-dominated right brain is just as valued as the logical and linear thinking of the male-dominated left brain. You live in a time where each human being has an opportunity to balance both hemispheres of the brain. This will lead to powerful human beings and is part of the new shift and the next evolutionary stage of humanity. All our lives lived as the women of this circle was in preparation for the new times. Without all of the previous generations' sacrifices, the world wouldn't be at the place it currently is. We are all one, coming from the same source. No matter if you live in the present time or, like us here in the circle, in the past, we are all in it together."

In Love

"I grew up a happy young woman and enjoyed my work as a nanny, taking care of rich people's children. I was in no hurry to get married, unlike the other girls of my age. It was not until my early twenties that I finally found the right man and fell head over heels in love with him, a handsome, popular young lad who swept me of my feet. He had had many girlfriends before me, but none of them stuck it out with him. My parents were concerned about what they had heard about him, and my twin sister warned me not to date the guy because of his sometimes radical behavior. But I, of course, ignored all their well-meaning advice, because I was convinced I could fix him. The young man had a lot of spunk in him, and he loved to entertain a crowd. Everyone would listen to his jokes. It was this lightness that attracted me to him, as I myself was shy and reserved. He was the catch of town. I felt that many girls envied me. I was determined to be his wife.

"And so I married Hillebrand Niewold in the year of 1886. Soon after our wedding, he changed from a jovial person to a depressed one who only lit up on the weekends, when he could entertain a crowd or seduce another woman. I carefully tried to share my spiritual beliefs with my husband, hoping he would change and see the light, but the young man thought my beliefs were rubbish and ridiculed me to such a degree that I learned to keep my mouth shut. It was safer that way. Plus my husband had plenty of talk for both of us, so I slowly lost my way of expressing myself. It was safer to hold my knowledge inside and pray in silence."

Domestic Violence

"Soon after we had children, the physical abuse started. First, Hillebrand mistreated and belittled me in front of others, but later he became more violent. I was exposed to daily physical abuse that got worse when he started to drink. I suffered tremendously, not understanding his behavior. Somehow I was able to protect my children from his brutal beatings and offered myself to be the only receiver of his rage and violence. He knew where to hit me so no one ever suspected what went on behind closed doors, as there was no proof. No one could see my bruises, because they were all hidden beneath my clothes. Afterward, he always apologized till the cows came home. In the beginning I fell for that, but after he'd broken his word of treating me better too many times, I lost all hope. After each beating, he showed remorse with tears in his eyes, but things never got better. Many times I thought back to the time before our marriage when my family warned me not to marry him. Now it was too late. Yet in my stubbornness, I would never admit it. My family, of course, knew what was happening in my marriage, but my pride and shame wouldn't allow them to help me, no matter how much they tried. I chose to be the perfect victim. Looking from the spirit side, I know how Hillebrand's struggles with the harsh life and hard work that had gotten the better of him. Over the years of our marriage, I allowed the light to be snuffed out of me. All I could do was make sure my children were fed and taken care of. Even in front of the children I was ridiculed by my own husband, who showed the kids to disrespect me in all ways. Fortunately it didn't stick; they knew better. I was too stubborn and too proud to ask for help, and kept all my pain inside as a well-kept secret. No one dared to reach out to me, as I was not the only one suffering; many women experienced the same type of abuse at home. The one thing that got me through the rough times was my connection with Mother Mary.

In secret I kept on praying every day, and whenever I could go, you would find me at church. Because I couldn't change my own situation at home, I prayed for others who I knew needed help or who were sick. Intuitively I knew if a woman was being battered like I was. She didn't have to say anything; I just recognized in her behavior that I knew so well myself. So all I could do was pray, which helped not only others but also me. This became a thing, especially later in my life, when I would pray for healing when people started to ask me to. And so I visualized their bodies becoming whole, being blessed with the grace of Jesus and Mother Mary. I had seen miracles happen that no one could explain, and I knew that it was not me who did the healing but the Holy Spirit that worked through me."

Widowed

"After our seventh child was born, your oma Klazina, my husband became very sick with a mysterious disease. He suffered for almost two years. Four months before I was to deliver our eighth child, Paulinus, Hillebrand died after a difficult journey. We were left broken both financially and emotionally. That's why I showed you the energy of a bird with a broken wing.

"Hard times approached when my children and I were dependent on the goodness of others to survive. A distant relative, an old bachelor uncle who needed help at his small farm, welcomed me to move in, along with the children who still lived at home. The work was hard, but I was so much happier being free from the brutal abuse of my late husband. In secret I considered myself lucky that he was gone. When I was thinking that way, I was ashamed of my thoughts. I was a single mother and a woman who had lived through two wars, and yet I still felt blessed with my life the way it was. Besides doing the farmwork, I slowly started my own garden growing vegetables, flowers, and herbs like my mother did. I made ointment from gathered beeswax and herbs and helped people with their ailments. Since I was free, I didn't have to hide my belief in God anymore. I could openly pray. I set up a circle with other women. We would pray in church for the sick. For many years I was bothered by the choice I had made to marry my abusive husband, which led to domestic violence. I had a difficult time trusting myself to make new decisions given the facts of my past. For a long time my wounds were deep, but somehow I was able to channel love and peace from the deepest parts of my psyche through prayer. Unfortunately, my children didn't share my love of being connected to the church. It had been communicated by their father, who didn't believe in any of 'this nonsense,' that there was no God a person could rely on. I died during the war in 1943, only five months before my youngest son, Paulinus, was murdered by the Germans. I thank God I was spared from the experience of that trauma."

Lessons: You Have a Choice

"One lesson I've learned from the domestic violence is that we can make a choice to stay or leave. Neither one is easy. It takes courage, determination, and strong will to make a difference. Fortunately, there are many places one can go to get help now. Many women marry a man whom they think they can fix and guide on the right path. This will never work. My advice is to walk away after the first beating, because it will not be the last, unless the abuser is willing to get help and do the work.

"Another important lesson I learned was not to swallow my pride but to admit to myself that I was wrong. Often we get in trouble because we are not honest to ourselves. I was too stubborn to admit there was a problem until it was too late, and then there was no way back. In my younger years I had the misconception that I could fix my husband and that everything would be peachy. In the process, I hurt both of us, him, because he knew he could never please me, and me, because with my limited mind I failed to change his behavior."

Guided Imagery: Finding Your True Colors

We were all sitting in circle surrounding Tressa and praying for guidance to release the emotions of domestic violence still present in so many women alive today. The energy of the community of women became intimate, and soon we chanted ancient songs with energy so powerful that we could see the colors dancing in the air, hear the sounds, and feel the vibration moving into our bodies. Then the women led Tressa to the creek nearby. When we arrived, we created a circle with our arms to cradle her in the shallow water. She floated in our midst and was slowly submerged in the water, washing away the memories of all women suffering domestic violence. The chanting continued, creating an even more powerful energy of love and peace. Tressa's field was now changing from an image of a bird with a broken wing to an angel with an eight-foot-wide field of rainbow lights. Her true colors were exposed, and in that light, darkness was nowhere to be found. Then the circle exploded into vibrant colors of light, a trillion beams of light, ascending into the sky. From there we drifted to the outer rim of the world, sending love and healing down to all people who suffer from violence. We witnessed the light being received by those in distress, bringing forth a new powerful way of making the right decision. I could feel in my own body how the victims of violence received this energy. Some felt a peace previously unknown coming over them. Others experienced healing vibrations of love in their hearts, moving through their bodies, and many felt a powerful clarity come over them, enabling them to make the right decision for themselves and their loved ones. After this powerful exhibition of light, we drifted back to our circle, where we found ourselves in silence by the fire, writing affirmations to finalize our healing session.

Affirmations

"I release old hurts of abuse and violence into the fire," spoke the voices in our midst.

With intent, I let go of the heaviness of negative experiences, not only for my ancestors and me but also for all humans, past, present, and future," said another voice.

The void that is created by the release of negative energy will be replaced and filled with love and compassion.

We are amid a new era on earth, a time of acceptance of our differences, a time of celebration for the new energy to come. I remember my connection with my spirit, and therefore I know that I'm a light being.

Note: If any of these affirmations feels right to you, reader, or if you think of some of your own that fit you better, please write them down in your own handwriting on an index card and say them out loud a couple of times a day.

Final Meeting

When we finished listening to Tressa's story, candles were lit and a celebration of releasing the energy of her experiences was offered to the fire. Through dancing, singing, and praying, the women came together in unity. Words of wisdom were spoken that rang with the power of love forcefully through the circle.

It was a sacred ceremony, filled with so much love that it freed us all from the dark ages that are now behind us. Dancing in a circle created a hue of light around us. I could almost feel us lifting up and covering the earth with a circle of light. A new door has opened, and all we have to do is walk through it with intent, love, and compassion.

After the ceremony, Oma spoke in a gentle voice to the entire circle. She shared her wisdom about the coming years. "First it will seem that there is more duality in the world. This is because if the light gets brighter, the darkness feels it's losing its power, which is true. That's why darkness acts out more violently, but in the end darkness cannot survive amid the brightness of light. Remember this, and consciously keep on shining your light and have compassion for your fellow humans."

Conclusion

A Look Back at the Journey

it all started with the diagnosis of breast cancer. My mind was on overload thinking about why this was happening to me. I started to contemplate why some people get cancer and others don't. Does it have anything to do with the way cells in our bodies respond to stress, foods, or the environment, or is there something hidden in our genes that emerges under certain circumstances? Of course I'm not a doctor or a scientist, but I am curious about discovering hidden mysteries. And that's what caused more questions to surface.

On my quest to find answers, the first thought to enter my mind was, *How do the memory cells of our DNA work with our genetic makeup?* My sister was diagnosed with brain cancer only three months before I was. Were these two cancers connected somehow through our genes in relation to our ancestors' experiences? Was there a possibility that we are our ancestors and so still carry diseases in our genes? Since my grandmothers often stressed that we are all one in spirit, I'm starting to wonder about that. If so, would that be the reason their energy felt so familiar? Then my mind wondered, what is my lesson on this earth? Have I chosen to be here at this time to make a difference and be part of the big shift everyone is talking about? Is this cancer a door for me to walk through and, once having done so, awaken to my true self?

The answer came in a dream the night after my lumpectomy surgery, when my grandmother's spirit paid me a visit. She was talking about the ancestors we share and how we are still connected through our genetic makeup. I was to meet them all soon in the dreamtime, as she called it. In meditation I was taken to the cedar grove where my ancestors would tell the stories of their lives one at a time.

And so the journey started. I explored the messages I received during the gatherings at the sacred circle. Here I met my ancestors, whom I lovingly call my grandmothers, who told the stories of their past lives. They shared how the emotional imprint of their lives, as well as their thoughts, are not felt by them anymore on the other side of the veil, but such is not the case for those of us who are alive today. We who are in physical form still deal with the emotions and the negative patterns recorded in our genetic makeup. Besides their sharing, my grandmothers prepared healing ceremonies for us to experience, guiding us to look at things from a different angle, and then release and let go of old beliefs. With that process, the vibration of our fields will be changed forever.

My grandmother spoke about the times we live in and the roles we are to play, in which there is no place for old, outdated behaviors. It's now a time of discovering how our thinking patterns shape our lives. When we shift to this new awareness, the negative behavior and the old ways of thinking will have to be resolved, making room for a new positive vibration of compassion felt all over the world. That's the reason for cleansing, releasing, and rejuvenating the cells of our DNA. Once we do this, our descendants will start with a clean blueprint. With a better understanding of who we are, we can look forward to the new energy to come.

Being present at the circle has healed layers of my own generational wounds, and listening to my ancestors tell their tales has cleared the records of our genetic line, past, present, and future. I feel blessed and humbled to have been the receiver of the amazing stories they shared with me. What I mostly learned from them was to recognize how everything that happens to me shapes my life in one way or another, depending how I process the issues at hand. Without my ancestors' wisdom, I would have been caught up, like many, in the daily dramas of today's world of dualities. With new understanding, I can shine light on the darkness of my experiences, a darkness that cannot exist where there is light. And so the cleansing of our ancestors' experiences recorded in the genetic makeup is now finished and will be replaced with a positive start for the seven future generations.

The Shift—a New Journey

We all have chosen to be here at this time to play our role of making the shift happen. With a little intuition, you can feel the changes hanging in the air. Humanity is awakening big-time, and yes, if you are reading this, you are part of this amazing movement. There is much potential hidden in our memory cells, and if we listen to the messages of our consciousness, we will gain clarity about our journey. We often make the mistake of thinking we have to do some big thing in order to make our life valuable. In realty all we need to do is to remember that we are light and to have compassion for others. That's how the vibration of our energy field will change. Being aware of the messages spirit sends us is key to changing the course of events.

To distinguish the messages from the mind/ego versus those from the spirit can be tricky. I suggest you pay attention to what the message feels like. If the information you receive is loving and only a few words or images are used, you are on the right track. On the other hand, if the message is negative with a lot of words, it probably comes from your ego/mind.

We can use our intuition as a guide to manifest goodness in this world. Stop being a victim. What happened to you in the past doesn't define you. Take care of yourself, meditate, relax your body, mind, and emotions, and remember that you are never alone; you are surrounded by the spirits of your ancestors, who love you. Generating this new awareness will change your world completely.

From now on my dear readers, be strong and follow your own intuition. Listen to what your higher spirit reveals to you. Trust the process, and be the light the world needs.

Guided Imagery: Transformation

To my surprise, I found myself once more among my ancestors whom I call my grandmothers. This time, however, we gathered on a sandy beach by the Pacific Ocean. It felt we were on one of the

Hawaiian Islands. One of the women spoke. "We have chosen this time and place of magic to do a final cleansing for all of you who have so patiently listened to our stories and, in the process, were affected in your emotional field big-time. We have noticed the colors in your field changing with each story told. Although you reaped the benefits from each healing that was presented to you, there is still some residue left that needs to be cleared."

I felt the fabric of my flowery dress caressing my body. The women took me close to the water, blessing me with sacred oils. After I was anointed, they carried me to the ocean and placed me gently in the water. I felt myself floating amid their circle. The salt water felt warm. Nearby, on the shore, I heard the traditional songs of ancient Hawaiian singers ringing through the air. Their drums and other instruments blended with the voices, calling the ancient spirits of their land. The sounds made my body vibrate with a pleasant feeling of being safe and loved by the land, the ocean, and the people surrounding me. In my arms I felt a strange sensation of something pushing against my skin. Next I realized two dolphins caressing me, placing their heads gently in the curve of my neck. ... For a moment my spirit drifted up above me and looked down at the scene below. I could see the entire picture of the women surrounding me, with the dolphins in our midst and in close proximity the ancient peoples' chanting. Words of support entered my mind. In a sacred way, I heard a voice speak.

"You are here to clear the old energies carried in your and all humans' genes from all ancient people who have walked this earth. From your grandmothers' spirits an extension is created to reach all people alive today. Your body is a conduit for the healing energy to be anchored into the world. We release old, outdated imprints from the blueprint of your being, as well as from the blueprint of all humans, and we free you from the darkness in your field."

I felt a wave of darkness moving from my body, dissolving into the water. Then a new wave of light was placed into my belly, and from there the energy moved into my heart, and then to my brain. It continued to travel into every single gene and memory cell of my DNA. I could clearly see and feel my body change to light. Then the dolphins caressed me again and nudged me with their noses. Next they swam away into the ocean. I could hear them say, "We will take this energy of new light around the globe." From my body, the light emerged from the water onto the land, reaching the ancient Hawaiian healers called kahunas. Their chants became even louder. I could see the energy moving over the land and through the air.

The next picture I saw was that of my grandmothers carrying me onto the beach and covering me with sand. "You will feel rejuvenated from this holy sand, and so will all others who experienced this ceremony. All they need to do is read or listen to the ceremony, knowing they are right there. This is for all who came to the earth with the purpose of making a difference." The warmth of the sun felt so good. I found myself drifting into a deep sleep.

When I awoke, I found myself in my eight-sided meditation building, remembering everything very vividly. I checked in with my body, which felt rested and rejuvenated. I wish for everyone who witnessed this ceremony to feel the same way and more. I know I am now free from the old ways of thinking as long as I make the right choices to walk away when I am confronted by someone who wants to draw me into their negative field. At those moments I will remember to breathe before I respond. It will take some adjustment to think positive, but we all have the power and the will to do so. And that's how we will change the course of humanity from a negative, outdated thought system to a positive, compassionate way of thinking.

Guided Meditation of Relaxation

You may use the following relaxation method prior to any of the guided imagery sections in *Visitors along My Cancer Journey*.

Start to focus on your breathing. Slowly inhale and slowly exhale. Keep your breath connected, and follow your breath as it moves into your lungs, expanding your chest. Take a couple of moments to focus on your breathing. Next, take your breath all the way into your lower abdomen, filling that sacred space with light.

Now imagine following your inhalation, bringing in light through the top of your head and moving into your brain, traveling down along your spinal cord. From there the light moves into every single cell of your body.

Next, start to relax your body, beginning at the top of your head. Relax the muscles of your scalp, the back of your head, and your forehead. Then relax all the muscles of your face.

Imagine the muscles of your neck and shoulders relaxing. If there is any stress you are holding in that area, release it and let it go. Let that stress be lifted from your neck and shoulders, up and away into the air, through the roof of the building. Visualize it being lifted up and drifting away, far away, lifting and drifting away from you.

Continue to focus on relaxing the muscles of the back of your neck and shoulders. From there, feel the relaxation move down your upper arms, elbows, forearms, wrists, and hands. From your hands, feel the relaxation move into your abdomen, followed by a calmness in the beating of your heart and the slow, calm breathing of your lungs.

Next relax the muscles of your entire back, first your upper back, then your middle back, and then your lower back. Feel the muscles of your buttocks and your hips relax. Thereafter, bring relaxation down into your legs—your upper legs, the area of your knees, back and front, your calves, your shins, your ankles, and your feet—until you are completely and totally relaxed."

When you are completely and totally relaxed, imagine yourself in your sacred place, a place of your choice.

About the Author

Klazina Dobbe was born in 1952 in the small country of the Netherlands. She immigrated in 1980 to the United States with her husband and their three small children. Together they started the Holland America farm in Washington State and later in California, growing flowers such as tulips, lilies, peonies and freesias. Both family farms are still greatly involved in the flower industry to this date. One of the greatest lessons Klazina learned from working with nature is that if you nurture a plant or bulb, it has the opportunity to blossom. When she began her journey as a healer, this idea became the basis of her healing practice.

Klazina's journey in alternative health care started in the late eighties with reiki and rebirthing. Ten years later, she earned a master's degree in acupuncture and oriental medicine at the Oregon College of Oriental Medicine. In addition, she became certified in hypnosis and NLP (neurolinguistic programming). Her training in different modalities, together with her intuition, led her to work with clients on their physical, mental, emotional, and spiritual bodies. For almost thirty years, she guided her patients to empower themselves and find the healer within. Klazina also hosts monthly meditation groups and teaches classes on awareness.

Printed in the United States
By Bookmasters